Memories and Reflections

A Refugee's Story

Edith Bown — Jacobowitz

To Stefan, with all my love

Printed in 11 point Book Antiqua

2014

Contents

1		Germany 1924 — 1939	3
2		Leaving Germany 1939	31
3		England 1939	35
4		My Diary and Correspondence	39
5		A Refugee's Story Continues	103
6		Appendices	
	1	Reminiscences: Apprenticeship of an Alien	109
	2	Fűr Das Kind	115
	3	Glossary	121
	4	Holocaust Day 2002	123
	5	The Jacobowitz/Gutman Fanily trees	127
	6	To Be a Pilgrim	129
	7	Gert Jacobowitz	131
	8	Return to Berlin	137
	9	The Pessach Song	147

1 GERMANY 1924 – 39

I promised to write down what I can remember of my early life, and those nearest to me. I like to think that it is because Stefan (my son), wants me to, to establish part of his identity. But in truth it is because I too am curious to remember the past, and keep the memory of so many I have loved. Perhaps the ones I think of are lucky, because through me they are remembered, if only with my eyes. Of the six million of my people that died, there must be many that have not one member of a family to remember them. But the main thing I wish to hand to Stefan is that his ancestors on my side were real people, with all the follies which this entails.

My father came from a family who originated in Poland. I think it was Katowice, a place that had coalmines. His birthplace was Fannygrube bei Laurahütte. The family name was Jacobowitz, not a rare one. My father's father had a public house near a mine, and owned pit ponies. He died young of pneumonia. According to my father, he developed this when rescuing casks of beer from a cellar which was flooded. He left behind his wife Ernestine, a beautiful but not very clever woman, and three children, a boy and two girls Hannah, Wilhelm and Else. My father told me that he had to leave the grammar school to start to earn a living. In one stage of his career he was a window dresser. He became so skilled that on one occasion, the rival store put down the shutters at his approach. Another story was that as a child he climbed out of the bedroom window and got on his sledge (they lived in Upper Silesia) to go for a ride. The village policeman got in his way, and they both went down to the bottom of the hill on my father's sledge.

I think my father was born a Pole, but became German by choice. This may sound peculiar, but at the end of the 19th century, there were still pogroms in Poland and Germany had a much more liberal reputation for Jews. When the First World War came, he volunteered, but was turned down at first. Later, he did get into the German army. By that time, I think, he was living in Berlin, working with an uncle. His mother and sisters were still in Breslau, where I think they had been for some time. Later on, they too made their home in Berlin. My father fought for Germany from 1915 to 1918. He was a private, then for some time a corporal. He lost the stripe for being rude to an officer. He was sent back from the front for a punishment. That saved his life. He told me that he sang at funerals of German and English soldiers. In 1918 he came back on leave to Berlin, expecting to be sent to the Italian front. He saw civil fighting during that time in Berlin, and vividly described snipers from the rooftops killing enemies and bystanders alike. On one occasion, he spent some time lying in the gutter, until one battle was over. Soon after that it was discovered that he had tuberculosis and he went away to a sanatorium, for a year at least, in the Tatra mountains. I have photographs and cards from that period. I also have pictures of him as a soldier in France. He never said much about the appalling conditions in the field. He had shrapnel in one knee, below the kneecap, which never ceased to give him trouble. He had to have it bandaged for the rest of his life. Every now and then, it broke down and festered.

Wilhelm Jacobowitz,
France 1916

His mother and sisters were now in Berlin. Here Tante Else married Emil Falkenburg, and Tante Hannah a catholic German by the name of Bernhardt. I make the last point specifically, in view of what happened later. Tante Else's children were James and Eva. Tante Hannah's children were four boys and one girl.

Else Gutman was my mother's maiden name. Her parents were first cousins. They came from Jastrow in West Prussia. My maternal grandmother was born in Topferstrasse; her maiden name was Simon, Emma Simon. Her mother's name was Henriette. These two families, the Gutmans and the Simons, had been in Germany for many generations. They were what was then known as assimilated Jews, having proper occupations. Grossmutter Gutman's father had been a baker. One of her uncles was a country doctor. In that family, even the girls were given an education.

Hermann & Emma Gutman

Grossmutter Gutman was a highly cultured and educated woman. I owe her a lot. Between her and my mother, I was influenced far beyond their deaths.

Herr and Frau Gutman moved to Dessau in Sachsen Anhalt after they were married. They opened a draper's shop. My grandmother was as much part of it as of her own household. When they had been married for some time, they had a house built in Kavalier Strasse 11. The shop was on the ground floor and there were another two floors above it. Their own quarters upstairs were not cramped but like the shop, were large and modern. They had the first house with central heating and electric light in the town. The architect used to say that he built the house with Frau Gutman. But, of course, they also had the old fashioned Kachelofen and the gaslight as well - just in case! The house stood on a big plot in the centre of the town. Part of the plot was sold by them later and the town's grammar school was built on it. Next to that was the Stadtpark, and across the road the theatre. The town Dessau had quite a cultural life; Moses Mendelssohn, the Jewish philosopher and liberal thinker was born there. His father was the cantor of the synagogue. The cantor's great grandson was the famous German composer, Mendelssohn-Bartholdy. During my own time, in the thirties, my grandmother had a second cousin in the town who did not live very far from her. Frau Weil used to worry about her son, Kurt, whose music and friends she could not understand.

My maternal grandparents had five children, one boy and four girls: Ernst, Meta, Hertha, Else and Gertrud. Ernst died just before the first World War, of a then unknown blood disease. He was about 19 years old. Hertha married Max Braunsberg and had two children, Hugo and Rosi. Meta did not marry; my grandmother did not want her to.

Else married Wilhelm Otto Jacobowitz (my parents) and had three children: Ernst, Edith and Gert. Ernst died before he was two years old, of tubercular meningitis, two weeks before Edith was born.

Trudchen (Gertrud) married Hans Jacobowitz, a cousin of Willy (Wilhelm) . She had one child, a daughter, Inge, but Trudchen unfortunately died about four months later.

There was an active Jewish community in the little town of Dessau. The Gutman children went to the local schools. My mother had a good education. All her life she used to say "If you have it in your head, no one can take it away, but they can possessions." All the children were taught music. My mother played the piano all her life. She had a lovely voice, which was to have been trained, but at eighteen she developed a gastric ulcer and spent a long time in bed.

She was tended by nuns from a nearby convent. My grandfather had been very generous to them. They felt for him, as he had recently lost his only son. They looked after my mother well. She told me that she remembered waking up and seeing the nun saying her rosary. Later, she went into a bank and worked there during the first World War. There she had her first experience of anti-Semitism. I have a letter which was written to me after the Second World War by an old friend of hers. I had met this woman's son as a prisoner of war by chance in 1946 in England. Her description of my mother was very touching. My mother was very sensitive and good. She was also very courageous. But more of that later.

My parents met when my mother visited her sister Hertha in Berlin. They went to the Braunsberg office, where my father had some business. Vati was a dashing looking young man. He had a lot of charm and was able to convey his personality. I believe my grandparents were not pleased with the friendship, and tried to nip it in the bud. There was a song in the twenties, "Schön ist der Junge, aber Gelt hat er nicht!" (He is good looking, but he has no money). He had had tuberculosis, and his side of the Jacobowitz family had nothing to recommend it. After they managed to get engaged, my grandmother Gutman's worst fears were confirmed. Vati's mother, Omama Tinka's home was in a seedy part of Berlin. Her domestic virtues were nil, her management worse. However, the rest of the Jacobowitz family were all gainfully employed in business. In fact, my father was not the only Jacobowitz to marry a Gutman. At my parent's wedding, my father's cousin, Hans, met my mother's youngest sister, Gertrud, known as Trudchen - and another match was made.

This is my parents' engagement picture. I got hold of it after 1945 and had it rephotographed. I have no picture of their wedding. My grandparents were able to give their daughters a good dowry. Of their sons-in-law, Max Braunsberg was the most successful one. He and his brothers set up factories in Frohburg, near Leipzig, weaving and printing cotton. One of his cousins or brothers married a favourite cousin of my mother's, named Tante Erna. She had three daughters and one son. The daughters survived.

My father had been in business with an uncle, but shortly after he married, he quarrelled with him, and no doubt with my mother's money, set up on his own. My parents eventually had a shop in the district of Gesundbrunnen, the Wedding, and a stall in the market.

My parents had three children : Ernst, Edith (myself) and Gert. We were all born in Berlin Charlottenburg, Wieland Strasse 8. Ernst was a well-loved, beautiful child and his death precipitated my birth. His nurse died at about the same time.

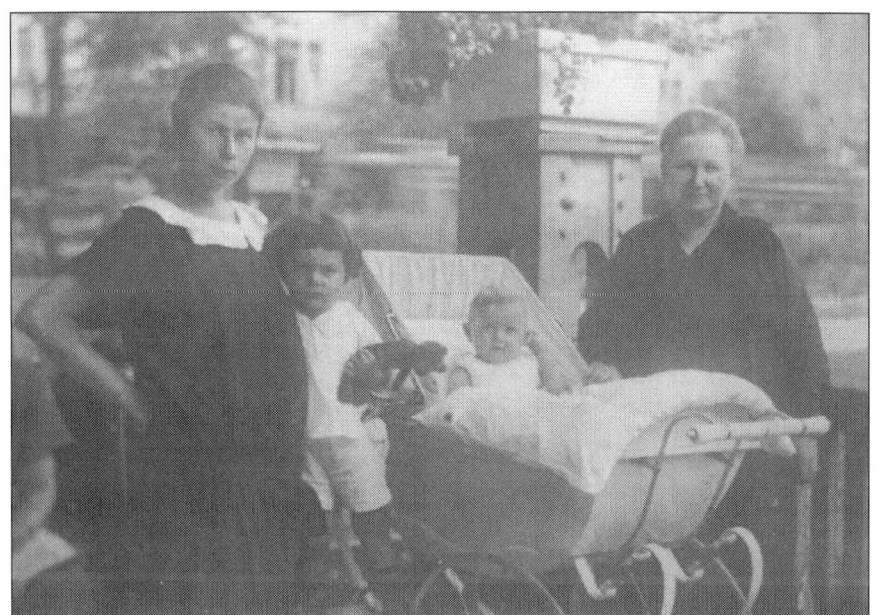

This is a picture of my mother, pregnant with me, holding Ernst by the hand, beside a pram with Inge in it, and Grossmutter Gutman on the other side. Earlier in that year of 1924, Inge's mother Trudchen, had died. Inge was about four months old when her mother died. Until her father married Trude Straschitz in 1927, Inge lived with the Braunsbergs and took over Rosi's last governess, Fraulein Gundelfinger. We played together a lot. Hugo, our older cousin was very much beloved by us. He seemed to understand small children. We had competitions, such as who could eat the most potatoes, or climb up trees the fastest. Inge always won! During that time Hugo and my mother became good friends.

I was a small, fretful child, difficult to rear, demanding for love and attention. My mother went back to the business to help my father, and I was left to Schwester Sophie, a trained children's nurse, not a nanny. My memories go back quite a long way: being pushed in a high pushchair, playing in a sandpit in the park, visiting my grandparents in Dessau. The flat in Wieland Strasse was on the first floor and had a balcony. The main railway line went past it.

Edith aged two
1926

My definite memories start from the age of four years. My grandparents and my mother went to Karlsbad in Czechoslovakia to take the waters. I fell down the stairs into the cellar of the hotel. I mistook the entrance for the stairs going up. (On reflection, two years later I turned out to be very shortsighted.) I remember going up in the lift with a cold compress on my head, my mother beside me. My mother was heavy with child (Gert), and attended a physician during her stay. I went with her, but I had no idea what it was about, though I knew all about the stork. When my brother was born a few months later, I upset everyone wanting to see 'where the stork had bitten Mutti.' The happy event took place at home, with a monthly nurse, my nurse, a cook and a maid.

Actually Gert was a very healthy boy, who never gave any cause for concern. I was allowed to hold him when he was a few hours old, which I liked a lot. At four years of age, I still had a bottle of cocoa at night! I went to the Kindergarten, and there I had my first taste of anti-Semitism at Easter, when one of the nurses acquainted me with the fact that as a Jew, I was not entitled to celebrate Easter with the others. The Kindergarten gave me whooping cough, six months after Gert was born. I gave it to the baby. We were both very ill. Schwester Sophie nursed us devotedly. We have pictures of the two of us on the balcony with Schwester Sophie. The year was 1929, in the middle of the depression. The weather was as cold and bitter as the economic situation. My mother told me later that people died in the streets. She did not let us out of the flat. The baby was dressed in outdoor clothes when taken through the corridor of the flat.

In the spring of 1930, we moved to Gesundbrunnen in Berlin. My father had one of his drapery shops there. He rented the two flats above it, and had them made into one. At the time he still had the stand in the local covered market and his shop at the 'Red Wedding,' which was in charge of his sister Else and her husband. James Falkenburg grew up there and his sister Eva was born there. Tante Else had only one kidney functioning , and was told not to have any more children after James. However, she ignored this advice and had Eva. After that she was never very well. She was always cheerful and in her, alas, short life always battled on. My mother used to help where she could, and Tante Else in her turn, used to help her sister Hannah. My father never forgave Hannah for her marriage. She was under the influence of her mother-in-law and became a Catholic when it was pointed out to her that her eldest child had died because she was a Jew. As she had four more children after that, God must have forgiven her. Her husband drank and chastised her.

We were not brought up as a 'politically conscious family,' but not all were blind to the political situation. Onkel Max Braunsberg died in 1932. Before he died, he told the family as a whole to pack their bags, take what they could, cut their losses, and go. The only one who did so was Onkel Hans Jacobowitz, who left for Holland with his wife and Inge, but that is another story.

I started school in 1930 at the local primary school. Like all the other Gutman grandchildren, I had my first satchel from the grandparents. My parents were respected in the area and I played with the children of other tradesmen in the street. It was discovered, on entering school, that I was very short-sighted, so I had my first glasses. I felt terrible; one or other people called me 'Brillenschlange' (glass snake).

My father became suddenly conscious that my Jewish education was neglected. He had become a member of the local liberal synagogue, and I was sent to the Jewish afternoon school twice a week. In Germany school started at 8am and finished at 1pm, so there was plenty of time to go to the Hebrew lessons and bible classes as well. On me, this had a mixed effect. I was proud of the

Conflicted identities

extra knowledge, at the same time I wanted to conform and be like the others. I have always said that if there had been no Hitler and fascism, there would not have been any Jews to speak of in another generation, so eager were the majority to be part of the national set-up.

My father went to the synagogue at New Year and the Day of Atonement, and on rare occasions on Saturday. He then left his sister and her husband to look after the shop. When I was older I taxed him with that, but was shouted down. This only confirms my opinion, that for sheer survival this schizophrenic, attitude had to go.

In the spring of the next year I went to the Gutman's for Easter and the Passover. My grandparents had sold the shop, but remained in the upstairs of the house.

My grandfather was an elder of the synagogue. I was honoured by reading the question asked at the beginning of every Seder: 'What makes this night so different from any other?' Of course this night had become a pointer to us, as it told about the flight from Egypt in the bible. This Passover Seder was organised by the Dessau Jewish community. There was a Jewish cabaret between the first and second part of the Seder. I fell asleep on the table shortly after saying my bit. No doubt it was the wine. I came to, to have my supper, but what I remember of the evening was a song, which was sung by the woman artist as part of the cabaret. It was an anti-war song, which left most of the adults in tears. At the time I could not understand it, but it had a lasting effect on me, especially as I heard a Yiddish version after the war from a boy who survived Auschwitz. I have written both the words and music down.

In 1931 and 1932 Schwester Sophie took Gert and myself to Storkow, not far from Berlin, where her father had a small-holding in the country. There we played with the farmer's children. Gert fell into a heap of pig manure, but was too sunburnt to be cleaned. They named a calf after me; I was very proud. We have a picture of that holiday.

Even my parents were worried by 1933. Onkel Hans, Trudel and Inge had left the country by then. That year (1933) I saw a voting booth for the first time, but from the outside only. That year, also, I saw my first picture, The Niebelungen. My father and I came in at the part where Siegfried is carried off on a bier. The result of the 1933 election in Germany started to change life. I remember the racists marching with torches, and the books that were burnt in the school grounds. My friends from the other shops ceased to play with me. When, unbeknown to my parents, I ventured into the shop of one girl's father I was shown the door in no uncertain terms. The teacher at school apologised to my parents for any insults to me, but said that in her form there would never be any trouble. I used to tell the class fairy tales when there was time, and when I ran out of the known ones, I made them up as I went along.

In 1933 business was bad. Hannah Bernhardt's husband and eldest sons made disturbances outside in Nazi uniform and demanded, and got, money to go away. Some of our astute friends and relatives left Germany. We had to give up the shop at the Gesundbrunnen. So we moved to Brunnenstrasse, further into the town, and I changed schools. Tante Else and her husband had to find other work and another flat, as my parents had only the one shop left now. The nurse had left when I was six years old and Gert two years. She was afraid for her reputation if she stayed with us, as Jews, any longer. 'Nothing personal, you understand'. The cook-maid went too. Tante Meta came to help at Brunnenstrasse. My father cycled from there to Gerichtsstrasse through the Humbold Hain, skirting the park. My mother followed on foot or by tram later, after sending us off to school. She took the dinner with her in tin cans every day. At school I identified with the only other Jewish girl. She was not a girl I would have ordinarily made friends with, but in the prevailing atmosphere it was inevitable.

At the beginning of 1934 life was becoming noticeably difficult. Many personal restrictions made themselves felt. The propaganda had trickled sufficiently into the people, and the children in my Junior School were aware of it. Some of their fathers could be seen in SA uniform. It gave them a certain amount of status. There was less unemployment, and regular marching of Brownshirts. Hitler's voice on the radio had become a habit. I never felt that so much as the vicious noise Goebbels made. Plenty of jokes were made about the dark-haired, ugly little man, who had an eye for the women, and whose reputation did not stand examination. His wife, Magda, had been the wife of a well-to-do Jewish man, who had employed him as a tutor. I do not know how true this is, but a Jewish wartime friend of my father's seemed to know all about it. Frau Goebbels produced one baby per year and was held up to be a good German woman. I remember once in the cinema, seeing a film of the 'Good Little Goebbels Children' cleaning their teeth. There was a lot of ribald noise under the cover of darkness. In broad daylight., of course, no one would have dared.

In the playground at school I started to be hounded, with the other Jewish girl. She might have been a scapegoat anyway. Her looks and smell of poverty, singled her out even in this school, which was in a working class area. But I tried to protect her, so I was part of it too. The atmosphere of antagonism in the classroom increased. During break-time, more than once, the Stuermer-inspired invectives were thrown at me. (Der Stuermer was the official paper of the Nazi party, mainly a paper of racism). 'Bloody Jew', cause of all our trouble, go back to your own country, if you are so clever, go die in the gutter, so very nice!

One day things came to a head. The teacher had to leave the classroom and appointed my chief tormentor to look after the class in his absence. The girl was to put anyone who talked against the wall to be dealt with by him on his return. The girl solved her problem by coming behind me and pinching me. When I said 'ouch,' she and one of her friends dragged me out of my desk and pushed me against the wall. When the teacher returned, he thanked her for her services, then turned to look at the culprits. When he saw me, he said: "You, I am surprised!" Whereupon I burst into tears, "It's only because I am a Jew. They mock me all the time, and she pinched me and when I said 'ouch' dragged me from my desk!" He slapped my face: "How dare you? What a lot of nonsense. No one would do such a thing here." He looked around the class, which had become silent, at his beaming guard, who had put me there. The silence swelled and he dismissed the class. I did not go to school next day.

My mother had wanted me to go to the Jewish School for some time, but my father, being a member of the 'Reichsbund Juedischer Frontsoldaten' felt that he was a German, and that all this demarcation was surely not meant for him or his family. He stormed to the headmaster, who informed him politely, that it was more than he dared to reprove the children. He was very sorry to lose a promising pupil, but I had better go. Soon after that, my brother had to leave the school. He had been attacked so often by bigger boys, that only his boxing skill had saved him from being beaten into pulp. So he went to the Jewish Boys' School near Alexanderplatz, and I to the Grosse Hamburger Strasse Mittelschule der Juedischen Gemeinde. Gert joined me there a few years later.

I must now tell the tale of Rosi Braunsberg as far as I can remember. Tante Hertha became rather like Queen Victoria after Onkel Max died, all black and very expensive. The big house in Berlin Gruenewald, in Fichte Strasse - now a mass of flats - had only herself, the staff and Rosi sometimes. Inge had left when Onkel Hans married again. Hugo had a life of his own. He came home sometimes, but always argued with his mother about money. The place was vast and very comfortable. I suppose I felt this more, as our circumstances diminished. A big natural garden, like a small park, a kitchen garden, quarters for the staff in the basement and the top floor, that was the picture. The
garages may have been horseboxes once. There were rooms rather in disrepair above them. In short, splendid for hide-and-seek. When all the family assembled it was fun. We children sat at the 'Katzentisch' , and were not supposed to listen to the grown-ups. But of course, we did. When it got really spicy, French or English was spoken.

Rosi was restless. She was 21 years old. I think she had been at a finishing school. She also had boyfriends no one approved of. At twenty she had run away to Switzerland to meet a man friend she had met at a girlfriend's house. His name was Gewuertz, later Girvan, and at that time he was a left-wing Socialist. He had made quite an impression on her. Hugo had brought her back; then off she went again to Switzerland. My mother and Tante Hertha went after her. They missed the train they were to go on, as Tante Hertha was late as usual. The train had a bad crash, and many people were killed. We did not know they had missed the train, for a day, and Hugo and my father were frantic.

A year later I was staying with Tante Hertha. Rosi was off to visit a friend. Hugo was taking her to the station, to make sure she got into the right train. Tante Hertha packed the clothes for her, for parties and fun. When she left the room, Rosi threw all that stuff out, and put workaday things into the cases instead. I watched but thought little of it at the time. Those two, mother and daughter, always quarrelled. Rosi had such a lovely suite of rooms. I always dreamt what I would do in her place. Well, Hugo saw her off, but a few days later the friend rang up to find out why she had not come. What everyone had overlooked was, that the last two carriages of the train went to Paris. Rosi stayed there with Toni Gewuertz until the German occupation. Toni managed to get by boat to England. He married her before he left and Rosi, by selling all her belongings, raised enough money to join a group of people who walked ever the mountains to Spain. There, by evading Franco's police, she managed to get into the British Embassy. From there she was flown to England.

About the time of Rosi's exit I was starting to learn English at school. While my mother was away in Switzerland I developed an ear infection in both ears. It was a most painful thing. In the end the specialist made a hole in my left eardrum so it would not burst. I was away from school for many weeks and lost a lot of ground. In the Jewish school there was much more competition. Whereas I had been in front of my form before, I now had to fight hard to keep even in the middle. German, history and music were alright, but arithmetic, Hebrew and physical exercises were appalling. My glasses did not help matters. They made me feel ugly and gawky. I enjoyed painting and writing stories and poetry. For the festival of Purim I wrote a play, completely in rhyme. But I missed the performance, as I had German measles. My mother had to lock the door, I was in such a rage. The whole class wrote me a letter, individual ones, but that did not make the blow any easier.

Else with Edith & Gert, 1937

In the years from 1937 to 1939, life went on; I went to school, my brother went to school. We had our lessons, did our homework, lived our private lives. If we were abused in the streets, accused in the papers and on the radio, our home was our haven and the family drew together. I cannot remember that our home life suffered, my mother did not let it. She used to get up at 6.30am get us up to travel to school on the bus and the underground. She tidied the flat with Tante Meta, cooked some food and set out on foot and tram to the shop. My father went on his bicycle. I used to go after school to the shop, but Gert came home to Tante Meta. There was a little room behind the shop, which had room for a deckchair. My parents used to take it in turn to rest there. We sold household linen, stockings, sewing articles and dresses. At one counter, leading to a corridor, was a big tie stand, after that was another bit of counter. There we had our midday meal. Then I had to go into the little room to do my homework. Along the corridor were shelves for goods. The corridor branched into two sections, one ended with the little room, which had a window looking into a dismal yard, part of a typical 'Mietskaserne'. The other part ended at a door to a toilet and facing it was a washbasin. My parents spent six days out of seven in this rather dingy, dark shop, mostly in artificial light, as the wooden backs of the shop windows excluded most of the light. My father used to make alterations to garments to earn a little more. Business was bad. James's parents fared much worse. They had a little flat towards the middle of the town: two rooms, and kitchen and bath. Onkel Emil often did not have any work and they supplemented their income by filling the place with lodgers. James used to help my father . On Saturdays we went out cycling, taking turns, James and I, on my father's bike.

After Schwester Sophie left us in 1933, Tante Meta came to us. She came to help my mother, who was working full time with my father in the shop. I would think my grandmother was responsible for this. Tante Meta slept in the nursery with my brother, I, in the maid's room. This had no windows, but was a space sandwiched between the dining room and my parent's bedroom. It had a window and a door into the corridor of the flat. The flat was on the fourth floor and took a lot of climbing. The flat was very spacious, only the utility rooms were mean, such as the kitchen and the bathroom. There was a big dining room, master bedroom, living room and nursery. I remember this as my home most of all.

All the time I went to school, and came back to the shop at the Wedding in Gerichts Strasse, so my mother could help me with my homework. My brother went back home to my aunt after school; <u>we did not get on and were always quarrelling</u>. I think he was teasing me, and I was a touchy child. He was a happy, healthy specimen, I was a thin, bespectacled girl, biting my nails, unable to either overcome my inner or outward failures. I was mediocre at school, except where reading and writing were concerned, but mathematics and languages eluded me.

If a teacher could get enough of a language into me so I was able to use it for expression, I would continue to learn; otherwise not bother. By the time I was twelve, all I wanted to do was to sit and dream or write, but of course, life was made of much more. The Mittelschule der Juedischen Gemeinde was not quite a grammar school, nevertheless, looking back on it, it touched on every aspect of education. It is difficult to imagine how the teachers, all Jews, coped with it all. The uncertainty of their own future, not only their livelihood, but their lives. They never knew if they would see their pupils the next day. If they were lucky, there might be a visa, and they could leave Germany without hindrance. Sometimes, when a child did not turn up, we knew that they had tried to get over the border by bribing the officials. And that might end in tragedy.

Under those circumstances we were taught languages. French, English, Hebrew, as well as geography, mathematics and history. The latter very carefully, so as not to offend anyone. Of course, there was Jewish history and religion. We had a gymnasium for sport and used an old unused graveyard as a racetrack. In this Jewish graveyard was a special plot for Thoras. It was the first time that I heard that old scrolls which are part of the Jewish service, were buried. Amongst our teachers was a very good music master, Herr Loewe, who must have hated teaching us. At times, he sat at the piano and played Beethoven and Mozart. Yet no one seemed to know. James went to this school as well, and we swapped tales. One day Herr Loewe became angry over the register. He poked his pen into the inkpot and it poured all over the register. The class tittered, and he exploded. Another time he lifted a chair in anger and broke it

I enjoyed history and read all the books I could get hold of. At my grandparents' house in Dessau there were many books, textbooks and novels with historical background. One thing which seemed to egg me on, was the need to understand the political situation. It seemed so senseless, this persecution of Jews. Even amongst Jews themselves, there seemed no unanimity of opinion. There were rich and poor, German, Polish and stateless, orthodox and liberal Jews. My father saw all in emotion, black and white; my mother just went on day by day, keeping all going and hoping. And I went on reading, listening, writing poetry and stories and trying to understand.

Sometimes, coming out of school, groups of jeering German children attacked us. We were asked by the principal of the school not to defend ourselves. On my way home one day, near the shop, a group of boys stopped me. They had catapults and pins, which they had bent. Before I could get away, they shot my left leg full with the pins. I ran the last lap to the shop. My mother saw what had happened and locked the door to stop my father going out. If he had touched the boys, he would have been arrested on the spot. I bled like a pig, when my mother removed the pins. My father had been good to these people and their children and was sorry for their economic plight. The shop was in a working-class district and he often let them off their debts, but when the people were told to boycott Jewish shops, they ignored it to the very end. Even when, after the 1938 pogrom, SA men were posted outside, some people still came into the shop.

At school, life went on as normal. I had few friends, hardly any. My mother made sure that I had the few cultural stimuli which were still available. There was one Jewish theatre which performed for schoolchildren. During the season I went, there was a ballot for the seats, so everyone had the chance to get a good one. There I had my introduction to Shakespeare, Voltaire and Lessing. I also heard one Opera: 'The Merry Wives of Windsor', by Nicolai.

Else, Edith & Gert at the Berlin Zoo, 1929

When I was a little child, we had a season ticket for the Berlin Zoo. Schwester Sophie used to take us there quite often. By 1938 one was not allowed as a Jew to go to the theatre, zoo and the opera. Even some streets were forbidden. The cinema had become an escape for my father. He spent many evenings there, to forget what was going on. The little cinema around the corner was very old. I was reminded of it by one in Paris many years later. But to go back to my father; suddenly he was not allowed to go to the cinema anymore. He then increased his smoking.

18.11.70. I would like, as this date spells Gert's 42nd birthday, to look back 32 years to his 10th birthday in 1938, in fact to go back to the week before that. 1938 was a bad year. Most of the ordinary privileges of the citizens had been removed from the Jewish population. Certain streets in the centre of Berlin were out of bounds. On certain national festive days it was not wise to go out at all. By the time the autumn came, all Jewish shops had to have special white painted names written on the windows. Some enterprising members of the Hitler Youth added slogans or stars of David. Others tried to intercept people from shopping.

In Paris, at the German Embassy, a young Jewish man, Hershel Greenspan, made his way in past the security guards, and shot a member of the Embassy, Von Rath. It was said that members of the young man's family had been sent to a concentration camp and this was his revenge. In Germany, it was rumoured that Von Rath had been an embarrassment for the Nazis, who had made it possible for the young Jew to shoot this man, thus getting rid of him, and using the occasion for a pogrom. We heard about this at lunchtime on the 8th November, and on the 9th, when the news of Von Rath's death came, I went out to fetch my brother from the barber. We went to a phone box, down the stairs to the entrance of the local U. Bahn and rang our parents at the shop. We asked them to come home, as we were sure something would happen. That night we did not sleep. The radio blurted out obscenities directed at Jews, Communists and other 'sub-humans'. We watched the jewellers across the road being smashed and looted by teenage Hitler youths, boys who were led by SA men. We were safe enough in our old-fashioned flat on the fourth floor. Our worry was for our shop at the Wedding. And then there were our friends along the road, who had a leather goods shop and a flat right behind it. In the morning we could see the broken glass all over the pavement, around the jewellers. In a way this was funny, as the shop had been acquired by a gentile owner only the day before.

The morning after 'Kristall Nacht' as the official propaganda version called it, I went to school as usual. In fact, I was the only member of the family to venture out. My mother liked to keep everything as normal as possible. I went by tram that morning. The conductor and the passengers were highly amused by the sight of broken shop windows. They applauded the looting as one way of getting even with the Jews. My eyes stung, as I listened silently to the abuse. When I arrived at school, I found my class halved. It appeared that all the people of Polish origin, with or without passports, had been rounded up during the night, and put on trains to the Polish frontier, and pushed into no man's land. We never saw them again. Let it be said for the teachers, that lessons took place for the rest of the day, without reference to what had happened. I spent the afternoon, after school, picking up the pieces of plate glass outside the shop of our friends. During the night the SA had broken into the shop, breaking windows, looting. Our friends had spent the night sitting on the steps of the staircase, behind their flat, as the looting had not been confined to the shop. None of the other tenants had dared to offer them shelter.

The next day our father went to our shop at the Wedding. We had a metal grill before the display windows, and in spite of the application of an axe, all the harm consisted of broken windows. No one actually managed to get through and loot. The months after November 1938 were very busy. By decree, my parents had to sell the shop. As it was a buyer's market, they only received about 2,000 Marks for it. That for the goodwill and the stock. It was the sweetshop owner across the road who bought it. I had purchased many a chocolate button there, and my father many bunches of flowers, which they sold as well. Just before November my father was approached by the Civil Defence people and asked if he would be an air raid warden in case of war. Already during the summer of 1938 Berlin had been prepared for air attack. On tall buildings there appeared anti-aircraft guns. Ordinary citizens were issued with gas masks, and the corners of the paving stones were painted white. To come back to my father and his invitation for air raid warden; he burst out laughing and said that he was very flattered, but did they really want a Jew? They had not thought of it, only looked up his war record.

From then on, my father tried in all seriousness to get us all out of the country. But to get out you needed money, and we did not have enough to qualify for any of the countries which would take you as a 'capitalist.' We had no connections anywhere outside Germany to qualify as next-of-kin. For America, the quota of German Jews allowed was over-subscribed for years to come, and for England you needed a guarantor and a labour permit, if you were over 14 years old. My mother had stayed in touch with a lady who used to call on us in the shop as a commercial traveller. She had gone to Northern Ireland, where her sister was married. My mother wrote to them on my brother's and my behalf to implore them to help us. My father was against this, as he did not want the family to be parted.

We celebrated the turn of 1938-39 in the usual way. My father made punch and our friends from the leather shop came. There were fireworks outside, the melting snow blocked the street drains and the road flooded. And we wondered about things to come. At the beginning of 1939, with the shop gone, my father was busy looking for a way out. My mother made plans for us children independently, and started to sell furniture to help us to live. She sold her beloved Bechstein Fluegel (grand piano) to a dealer downstairs and received 100 Marks for it. Soon after that every bit of silver in the flat, apart from two sets of knife, fork, spoon, etc. had to be handed in by all the Jews. My mother kept an eggcup and spoon belonging to my eldest brother as a memento. Life was a kind of no man's land. At the beginning of May my cousin Hugo was released from concentration camp. He, his uncles, and his cousins, who had all been there, had to sign all their property away to get out.

On the 5th May in the afternoon I came home from school, and found my parents, my Aunt Meta, in the company of two men. As I opened the door I heard my father say 'surely not there, it is only the room of a schoolgirl! ' It was the little room which looked out into the corridor, which they were searching. The rest of the flat had already been searched.

Sometime in the morning the two men called, asking for my father, but he was out. They said that they would come back later. My mother sent my Aunt Meta downstairs with money and a passport to tell my father to clear out, and try and cross the border of Germany somehow. My father had refused to do this, in case it put the rest of the family into danger. So he sent Aunt Meta to phone his friends and my mother's nephew, Hugo, who had just returned from Sachsenhausen concentration camp. My father then came upstairs to face what was coming. The men came back in the early afternoon, found my mother burning papers and stopped her. They turned the flat upside down. They found a few silver trinkets which my mother had kept, gifts to her eldest son. Since all silver had had to be handed over some months previously, the men took them. They found 1,000 Marks in my Aunt's suitcase. My mother had given it to her. That was all that was left over from the forced sale of the shop. When the men searched Aunt Meta's case, she claimed the money as hers, then my mother said it was hers. 'Bloody liars, the lot of you' was the comment. They confiscated the money. By the time I came home all was in confusion. My brother had returned earlier from school and was standing there. My aunt was crying. An hour after I came home the men went off. They told my father and mother to get a few things together. My father blanched and said "Surely not my wife, when you have got me?" The men just told him to shut up. Until now my mother had been calm. Now she started to sob. She put her coat on sobbing, and with my father and the two men left sobbing. We, Gert, Aunt Meta and I kissed them, and my father said to me: "Look after the boy, promise!" I promised. Then the men asked my father how to get to the police prison at Alexanderplatz. My father told them that the best way was by Underground. So they all went, my parents in front, the men behind them. I saw them from the fourth floor window. My brother nearly fell out of the window. We were left in shambles.

As soon as my parents were gone, my aunt became very distressed. I went out and phoned Hugo, who had known that something drastic was going on. He came and took charge of the situation. Next morning my brother and I went to our school to acquaint them with the situation. As this was an everyday occurrence in the Jewish school, they quite understood that I would need some time off to contact the authorities. So at 11am I presented myself at the prison at Alexanderplatz and joined a queue of relatives who were engaged on the same business as myself. I had taken with me my parents' toilet articles and other needful items.

Of the days that passed, I have only a very hazy memory. Hugo tried to find out why my father and mother had been arrested. It could not be because we still had any money, as the money which the men found in my aunt's case was the last between us and starvation. I went to Alexanderplatz every morning and from there to school. Every morning I tried to get some information, and every morning I came away without it.

At the end of the first week I had a letter from each of my parents on prison paper, asking for warm clothes, underwear and my mother asked for knitting needles and wool. She made me two long-sleeved pullovers during her ten months in prison, but was never able to send them to me. Hugo took charge of us. He decided that we must give up our flat, pack our trunks, store what furniture there was left and move in with his mother, Tante Hertha, who lived near the Gruenewald. He also encouraged me to write to Northern Ireland to hurry our emigration. My mother had started on this prior to her arrest, not telling my father much about it. He did not want us to be split up! So I now wrote to the Chairman, Mr Hurwitz, of the Jewish Community in Northern Ireland, explaining our plight and begged him to hurry up our escape from Germany. Hugo assured me, that that would be what my mother wanted for her peace of mind.

One morning, when I went to the prison to bring a parcel of necessities, a very young police officer received me and took the parcel. "Don't be too upset" he said, "I'm very sorry about this, but we are not all bad." This rather upset me, as I was used to the callousness and indifference, even from other people who came to the prison for the same purpose. They were too busy with their own misery to care for anyone else.

At last we found out what sparked off the search and arrest of my parents. Someone had been caught crossing the Dutch border, and he had an address book on him. Every name in the book had been sought out and the people picked up.

We started to wind up our home and move to my Aunt Hertha. Gert and I continued to go to school from her. It was quite a long way by train and we had to stay for school meals. In the meantime my parents had been moved to a prison in Fuhlsbuttel, near Hamburg. At the time I was 14½ years old and Gert was 9½ years old. The winding up of a home is not an easy task at any time. Hugo suggested that I should go ahead and try to arrange for Gert and myself to get out with one of the children's transports. This involved quite a lot of running around to various authorities, even after it became certain that the Jewish Community in Belfast were willing to vouch for us.

Hugo insisted on taking us to see our grandparents in Dessau. He made us promise not to tell them what had happened to our parents, but make believe that they had left the country and crossed the border into a neighbouring country 'black', as we called it. As by that time, Gert and I were assured of leaving Germany within the next three weeks, it was also to be a farewell visit.

Grossmutter Gutman
1938

My grandfather was getting senile; I think that the events had taken their toll. Only three years before, he and my grandmother had celebrated their Golden Wedding with all the family around them. Now only my grandmother was able to cope with events. She had ever been the moving spirit and could now see with icy clarity what was happening. Over that weekend, in tears, she implored me again and again to tell her what had really happened. She loved my mother ever best, as she was the nearest to her. And my mother had had the hardest life of all her daughters. But I stuck to the agreed tale, and left her uncertain. I cannot remember our leave-taking, which my grandfather did not understand, but Grossmutter Gutman did.

Before the storm: the Gutmans' Golden Wedding, 1937

Back in Berlin, I had to arrange to collect the necessary documents and permissions to leave the country. On one such occasion I remember a big hall in one of the Jewish buildings. All around there were stands with German officials, who examined the various parts of the exit passes, and made sure you were left with nothing on leaving the country. In the ante-room, where people assembled, an old woman was sitting, sobbing loudly: "My son is in a concentration camp, will no one help him to get out?" Past her moved a silent queue of cowed people, like the static wailing wall in Jerusalem. When I told Hugo about it later, he said: "Let that be a lesson to you, no one cares what happens. That is the world and never tell the world about yourself."

A first cousin of my mother, Tante Erna Braunsberg, came to Berlin to shop with me. She had four children of her own, who by good foresight had already left the country. Her daughters were in England at school, but her only son went to Belgium. As we went shopping to the best shops, and I am sure she paid for it all, she said: "We must send two well fitted out children into the world." She kept her tears in check at my mother's fate. They had been close friends in their youth, both Gutman girls, but Erna had married one of the Braunsberg cousins, the same family as my Aunt Hertha, and they had become very prosperous. So here she was, helping me to get ready.

In the meantime I applied for permission to see my parents before we went. We were now getting letters from them, full of love and a lot of admonition from my father.

At last the day of our departure with a children's transport was fixed. It was for the 20th June. I had with help and suggestions packed two travel baskets. They were huge, like hospital baskets. It had been Hugo's idea. The baskets were waterproof lined. Into them went our clothes and as much household linen as could be got into it. We were sending them to Ireland via Belgium. Of course, the authorities had to have duplicate lists of everything. It all took a great deal of time, but that was not the greatest of my worries. I had been asked for an interview by the Security Police at the headquarters in Herman Goering Strasse. The name of the building escapes me. Sufficient to say, that this one, and many others near Unter den Linden, not far from the Brandeburger Tor, were very much out of bounds for Jews. I therefore needed, and was given, a special pass. None of my older relatives could come with me. They wondered if they would see me again. So off I went to Herman Goering Strasse, clutching my piece of paper. Hugo had said that even if I were frightened, it was my duty to my parents to face this ordeal. It was one of these huge U-shaped entrances with a sentry box. In it a tall SS man examined my papers and waved me on to a young SS man who made me follow him. We went through passages never ending. At the beginning, the building was most imposing with grand doors. The man stopped in front of one of them and knocked. It was a huge office full of carpet. He clicked his heels and saluted, introduced me. The man behind the desk took a cursory look at me, and waved us on. So we went out and continued to walk to a part of the building which looked most business-like. The typewriters were busy and telephones rang. In the end, we walked up a narrow staircase and entered an office, where a typist was sitting. She stopped and looked up. The SS man gave her my pass and papers, told her to ring him when they were finished with me, and went out.

I don't know how long I sat there in that office and waited. The typist took no notice of me and I was too apprehensive to talk. I had dressed myself to look young and plain. Rumours about the cruel treatment of pretty women had dictated this. And I looked plain and drawn after a month of suspense and fear.

After some time I was asked into the adjoining office. Two men were sitting there. I was offered a chair, and they began the discussion. Mainly about my wanting to see the parents, and slowly coming to the point of their arrest. They asked me if I knew anything about my father's movements of the last few months, how we lived, and where I thought the money was coming from. If I remember right, I answered as simply as I could. I said that my father was trying to get a visa to somewhere and that we lived on the money from the sale of the business. The same questions were repeated in various forms to lead to a specific answer. I was aware of this all the time and never varied the answers. At last they asked me why I wanted to see my parents, and I explained that my brother and I were leaving Germany in about ten days. They promised to see if they could help me, and the interview was over. The SS man conducted me through the convoluted corridors of the building and I had to give up my pass at the entrance.
As soon as I was outside the forbidden area, I went to a phone box and rang Hugo. He seemed relieved. During the short time we stayed at his mother's flat, Hugo tried to prepare us for our

Preparation

forthcoming stay in England. We had cornflakes and porridge in the morning and tea with milk. A teacher from my school was engaged for extra English lessons, and I manfully ploughed my way through 'David Copperfield' with the help of a dictionary. All this activity was carefully planned to keep us from thinking too much.

2 LEAVING GERMANY 1939

The morning of our departure arrived, and so did a letter from my mother, from Fuhlsbuttel. I sat in the taxi reading it, with a kind of numbness which follows a crushed hope. We were not to see our parents again. To the station came Tante Hertha, Tante Meta and Hugo. It was early in the morning, but there were so many children between the ages of six months and fourteen years. All the younger ones travelled on a group permit. I was one of the eldest and actually had a passport. My brother was on the group permit. This was one of the last 'Kindertransports.' About 10,000 children were saved that way. There were about 150 children in the charge of English Quaker ladies. What a task it must have been for them. We each had a ticket around our neck, with our name and destination. I think we went from Bahnhof Friedrichstrasse. Part of a train was allocated to us. We were settled into our compartments after embracing our relatives and friends. The train then started on a slow journey out of Berlin. So slow was it, that many of the relatives took a taxi from station to station to see their children slowly going by. Tante Meta was amongst them. We passed the house in Charlottenburg, Wielandstrasse 8, where Gert and I had been born. We passed the still-smouldering synagogue in the Fasanenstrasse. Then the train left the city. I wore a grey costume, pink knee length socks, blue shoes and a pale blue hat with a wide brim. I ripped my new skirt in the first hour. I do remember how distressed I was, and how important it seemed. I talked to the girl sitting opposite me. She was going to relatives in England. I was envious, for we were going to strangers, into the unknown. The train was stopped at Aachen, and it seemed as if the uniformed men, SA or SS, wanted to search us and all the older children with passports. We were to leave the train, and I was petrified, as I had several undeclared trinkets with me. One was an alarm clock Hugo had given me the previous year. However, the ladies of the party kept the SS or SA men arguing, until with German punctuality the train started up again. The ladies waited till it moved and then jumped into the compartment, but not till we crossed the border were we safe. I had expected a great feeling of relief at being safe at last, but it did not happen. At Utrecht, the first Dutch station, the train stopped, and we were amazed to see the platform full of people with bags, baskets of flowers and gifts. And that was for us. Several babies left the train . In Amsterdam there were more women to greet us, amongst them Tante Liese Hogenhuis and Tante Grete Korthals. These were cousins of my father. They cried. I did not understand. What had they to cry about? I had to tell them what happened to the parents. They put bags of fruit and food into my and my brother's hands, and the train went on to The Hook. In passing, I must say that more children left the train in Amsterdam. Most of them were caught up in the transports to the concentration camps after the Germans invaded Holland.

We embarked on to a ship at Hook van Holland. I was fortunate in being allocated a cabin of my own. In my mind I was quite sure that I was going to be sick, and that all night. So I climbed into the top berth and prepared myself for the ordeal, putting water into a glass and a paper bag by the bed to be ready. I thought that the top bunk would be better for being sick. I must have fallen asleep very quickly from the faint rocking of the boat. When I woke up it was about 6 am the next morning. I got up and dressed and found my way to the top deck of the boat, in time to see it draw into Harwich. But it was not time to embark yet, and we had to wait for over two hours to go through the customs. In the meantime we went to the dining room for breakfast. I cannot remember what we were given, except for one item, white bread, and as I had never seen or eaten such before, it made a great impression.

At long last we were able to leave the ship and to go to the empty platform. We had apparently missed the train which had been booked for us. When at last a train arrived, we were grateful, as there had been a fine rain all the time. The journey to London seemed endless, and by that time rumours were going round, that we would be distributed when we got there. I had such terrible visions of being parted from Gert all along. We arrived at Liverpool Street Station and were ushered into a large hall. There were chairs in rows, and we were told to sit down till we were asked for. People were coming in to talk to the ladies who had conducted us this far. Then the name and the number of a child were called out and the child went. At best some of my travel companions knew the people who called for them, at worst children were crying as they were being parted from their brothers or sisters. It was explained to them that it was only a temporary measure, but they were too distraught to listen. We were there till the end, and my fears grew. Were we going to be parted, or equally bad, forgotten. Life at a railway station seemed no consolation after Germany. Then a very charming middle-aged lady came, and Gert and I went with her in a car. It turned out that she was the sister of the President of the Jewish community in Belfast. We were to stay with her till it was time for us to catch the train to Liverpool. The car seemed to go through endless streets of little red-brick - houses. It was explained to us that in England people lived in houses rather than flats. We arrived at last at the semi-detached home of our hostess. It was a large house in what I now know to have been a very middle-class area. We were sent upstairs to the bathroom, and then taken to the dining room. At the table we were introduced to a handsome, curly-headed boy of about 10. 'This is Felix Süssman,' said our hostess, 'He came by plane from Czechoslovakia. After lunch we were put into the car again and then into the train from Euston to Liverpool. Our hostess handed us each a bag of food and a drink, gave us into the porter's charge and waved us off. I cannot describe the feeling of desolation which assailed me, the dread of the unknown and the straitjacket of an inability to communicate. Fortunately, Gert was not so impressed, or shall I say, depressed by our surroundings. He made faces at all the people in the carriage and accepted food from them. I was embarrassed and told him off, but that was my way of letting off steam. The journey seemed endless.

3   ENGLAND   1939

On our arrival at Liverpool Lime Street Station, we were met by a gentleman who spoke some German, and was therefore able to allay some of my fears. It was not that I did not know any English, but the people in the railway carriage and the porter did not understand me, and I was not able to understand them. So at Liverpool we were taken from Lime Street Station to the docks for another overnight ferry, Our benefactor tried to get us a cabin to sleep in, but he had not booked one, so he slipped a tip into the purser's hand, handed me the money and left the ship. There I was on the deck with four pieces of luggage and Gert. He had become very frustrated and was now determined to get about a bit. He, therefore, disappeared up a ladder to another deck, always shouting 'yoo-hoo'. The hunt was on, as I tried to follow him up and down the decks! Finally, I caught up with him and by that time a cabin had been found for us. I felt happier when we both went into it and I could close the door on to the outside world. I remember insisting on us both washing ourselves thoroughly so that we would arrive in a respectable state, wherever we were going. At the time I had no idea where. That it was Ireland, I had completely forgotten. I was full of fear of the future and the misery of the past. The loss of my mother and my fears for her and my father, at the same time the feeling of guilt that I had left them behind to perish! We had tea and biscuits in our cabin next morning. I was not sure that my money would stretch to breakfast. When the ship berthed we went on deck with our luggage. It was raining. We must have looked a funny sight. My grey costume, pink knee socks, blue shoes and a blue felt hat, were what the well-dressed girl on the continent wore, but were completely out of place in Ireland. Gert wore a suit with short trousers, his hair was very short. And it never stopped raining!

Mr Hurwitz came to meet us and gave us a bear hug and in Yiddish welcomed us to freedom. Whereupon I burst into tears, and Gert laughed. Then my beautiful hat blew off my head, and was hardly recognisable by the time I caught it. It seemed to amuse all the others, but was a sad omen to me. Then we drove through grey

Edith & Gert with Barney Hurwitz, Millisle 1943

streets, that were dirty and wet, streets with mean redbrick houses, tall narrow houses with small stone walls around non-existent front gardens. When we stopped in front of one of these houses my heart sank. The door opened and a dark-haired excitable lady greeted us and our conveyors in a foreign language. I was nonplussed when Mr Hurwitz seemed to expect us to answer. What was a pattern of sounds was repeated and some of it had a familiar ring. At last I realised, it was a form of German, in fact, it was the equivalent of Berlin dialect, only this was Viennese.

The house to which we had come was a tall red-brick building, semi-detached, but it might as well have been terraced when the proximity of the other houses was considered. It was in a very respectable street.

The Rabbi, J. Schachter, lived just across the road, at 101 Clifton Park Avenue. The Jewish community of Belfast was not very large. There were about 100 householders, most of them second generation in the country. Their parents had come from Russia, Romania and Poland. All had been the victims of anti-Jewish pogroms and other racist violence. Their children, the present generation, had been imbued with the past, so that this small group had vouched for a hundred Austrian and German Jews, to save their lives. I think that they did this without thinking any further, but just getting people over, having the terrible task of refusing refuge when they were saturated. Every refugee had to be signed for and I believe £100 had to be put against each one, as surety not to become a burden on the rest of the non-Jewish community. So there we were. The house was a refugee hostel; downstairs there were a kitchen, a scullery, a sitting and a dining room; on the first floor were the bedroom of the matron and a large front room used for the girls and older women. It held between six and ten beds. It meant that it was very crowded, no room for a chair or bedside table. Certainly no room to unpack. The floor also had the one bathroom and toilet. On the second floor there were two rooms, a small one for two students, who were able to study as they had arrived with money, the other big front room was for the boys and unattached young men.

If I had expected a warm welcome from my refugee 'mates' I was mistaken, but at that time, once having left Germany, I felt confident of nothing but goodwill elsewhere. Unbeknown to me there had always been friction between Austrian, German and Polish Jews. The further West you went in fact, the more the educated Jews used to look down on their brethren from the East. Apart from the fact that over the generations, Jews in each particular country had acquired the outlook and habits of the country they lived in, and were as prejudiced as other nationals. So once the immediate threat of Jewish liquidation was removed, the old jealousies revived. The hostel was full of Austrians, and we were only the second group of Germans to arrive. The matron, a rather garrulous woman, told the committee that there was room for us, but hoped that there would not be many more. Gert and I were put into our dormitories. I was told that we had to take turns with housework, which included cleaning and washing-up.

The house was cold and damp, the sitting room only used by the adults, who kept the children without parents in their places and managed to make themselves comfortable. The allocation of housework was also dependent on who you were. Mind you, they never had any luck when it was my turn to light the fire. Occasionally we were invited out to tea with a member of the Jewish community. But I remember one afternoon, when just as we were going to sit down to tea, the lady of the house said: 'But your parents must have done something to be in prison.' The more enjoyable visits were to the house of our guardian, Mr Hurwitz. His wife had a heart of gold and always made us feel good. Of course the lady, Miss Perilman, through whose introduction we owed our lives, used to invite us as well to her sister's home. There we found something like a German household, but we were always reminded of our duty and gratefulness to the people in Belfast. All this took place at the beginning of the summer of 1939. It rained most of the time, and it was cold. From the window of the bedroom I watched unending funeral processions. It must have been the main road to the graveyard. I once asked why there were so many funerals, and was told that they all died of rheumatism!

4   MY DIARY AND CORRESPONDENCE

What I have written so far was the start of my memories, dating from 1971. Since then, I have been able to find letters dating back to 1939. The other item which will help me to recall memories of fifty years ago is the diary which Hugo gave me on the 16th September 1938, my 14th birthday. Much of what I am writing has already been recorded in the first part. It may help to make the letters and the diary more understandable. On the other hand, the letters and the diary carry over to the time when the war actually started.

It was on 16th September 1938 that I was given a proper leather diary by cousin Hugo for my fourteenth birthday. Of course, I lost the key on the first day, so it was not till the 21st that I started to record what seemed important to me at the time. I continued to do so for the next two and a half years, up to March 1941. It is difficult now to realise that during that time the whole of my family life, my home, and the world around me, was destroyed. True to form, the diary is started on the day I managed to prise it open and it has a picture of myself on the first page. Also true to form, school plays an important part. There are class, politics, and of course - love. I was in love with cousin Hugo, at least twelve years older than me. He was a sophisticated young man, whose fondness for my mother rubbed off on me, like a puppy. His own mother, my mother's elder sister, was an unworldly, spoilt woman, who did not understand the political and economic situation. At the time of my birthday, my parents still had the draper's shop. There, in spite of our being known as Jews, the people still came to the shop.

The Diary Begins

21 September 1938

At last I have been able to open the book, though I managed to tear the leather catch. Today the 'puppet', (our small, malformed music master) complimented the PE mistress, but remarked that she had so many girls sitting idle. 'Herr Lowe' she said 'Don't you know anything about the menses ?' He went purple, and we laughed. This afternoon at home the lights fused. Gert, the devil, repaired it. The two Ilse's at school have many secrets, they want to raise Ruth's and my curiosity. Yet they say bad things about her. Friends ! (I still have pictures of all of them).

26 September 1938

Rosh Hashana, a great day for me. When I left the temple I felt so much easier.

27 September 1938

What does it matter. Rosh Hashana (the Jewish New Year) is over. I am so afraid for Hugo because I love him so. I am crying for him, oh God! My head is beating. I am fourteen years old and two weeks. I will promise myself never to love any man and make it my task to be as beautiful as possible.

3 October 1938

Kol Nidre (the Day of Atonement). We had a great shock. Tante Hertha and Hugo had a car crash. She broke her hip and thighbone. Hugo broke some ribs and was in shock. Vati fell and sprained his leg. He is much better. He is at home. Hugo is looking very ill.

14 October 1938

A visit to my grandparents in Dessau. I have been in Dessau these last six days. Yesterday I went to the cinema. Nearly every afternoon I am doing something different... No advance in our emigration prospects. Odd, they want to get rid of us, but lock us up. Hugo looked bad yesterday. (He had been taken to a K.Z.) Oh dear, the last week.

27 October 1938

Yesterday we had a new teacher, Miss Heikman. Ruth

Oppenheimer tells me that she is hoping to leave this year or at the beginning of the next year to go to the USA. One after the other is leaving. We have not seen Hugo for a long time. The Jacobowitzes from Palestine have not written since our New Year. God protect us. Schema Yisrael.

The next entry was after the shooting of Von Rath in Paris.

7 November 1938

I am very tired today. (Dead) nearly from all the excitement. I am so afraid. Tante Hertha is not well. My dear friends and I are keeping together. I wanted to make chocolate.

15 December 1938

Today Hugo was with us. He has at last left the sanatorium (KZ). He is looking so well that I was quite surprised. Tomorrow I am visiting Tante Hertha at home. She is limping a little. Our furniture, the dining room and bedroom, we have sold. About the shop a decision will be made soon. We have put our name down for help regarding emigration. I hope something will happen soon. Either Holland or England. But man thinks and God decides. It is Channuka tomorrow.

12 January 1939

Oh, the first entry in the new year. Of course, not for us Jews. Never mind. Today I stayed at school in the afternoon for the first time. We, my friend Ruth and I, rang Inge (another friend). Then Ruth bought Herring Salad and I a pickled cucumber, as well as two bread rolls.

25 January 1939

How disappointed one can be. Hugo made me quite sick. He insisted that my parents had done something wrong. But Mutti has explained it all. A lot of nonsense. I am trying all the time to forget about our despair. One is so very nervous. Today I was not at school.

4 April 1939

For a change today we have applied for papers to Australia. There is a 90 to 100 per cent possibility that it might work in six months. Pessach has started. Unfortunately I could not go to Dessau. Grandmother has a bad cold. Vati and Gert went to the synagogue, one of the few still in existence. Now at last I have finished my official school years. The report was not good. I don't care. In eight to ten days James Falkenburg is going to England. He will stay there for two years. Then he will go on to Palestine. This morning I was reading for the umpteenth time: 'Katherine becomes a Soldier'. I wish that I could be like her. Her parents were so stupid. In their eyes she was lower than her friend, the stupid Jeanne. I worked it out, that Katherine was as old as Mutti. The holidays are so boring. One cannot go anywhere. All the time the same walk to our friends, that is the parents. All the other girls at least have their friends. How is it that I am always alone? I was so disappointed with Ruth Oppenheim.

29 April 1939

At last there was an answer from Ireland. They have asked for the permit. Mutti is reassured. Today I went out with Aunt Luz. I found the walking about quite tiring. Well, one learns something every day. James is now in Scotland for two weeks. The farewell was very merry. Tante Else is so happy. There are now only a few girls left in our class. Gert has started at our school and has had his first English lesson. Ruth 0. is in Brussels. She goes to school there. I must write to Inge and James soon. -

5 May 1939

Today and yesterday I stayed home for a change. We have been buying many things. I dream of a journey at night. I hope it comes off. Tante Meta is with us again.
The other day I wrote a happy letter to James. Inge received a card.

The day after this entry my parents were arrested. Between then and until I arrived in Northern Ireland, nothing was written.

In Northern Ireland.

22 June 1939

The day before yesterday we left Berlin. It was hard to go without saying goodbye to my parents. It is now six weeks since they were fetched. In the middle of working and thinking. We travelled from Berlin-Bentheim-Harwich-London- Liverpool-Belfast. Now we are in a hostel. I would have refused to come to this if I had known before. But like this I am faced with a fact. Gert is very happy. He likes to be with a lot of people. Now I must write how it all happened. The community in Belfast does a lot for German Jews, although there are only 1,000 people. Most of the children, about 105, were taken into families. About 25, amongst them us, are here in a hostel. The children in this hostel have all been vouched for by Mr Hurwitz. There is very little room here. I can't even unpack my suitcase. The clothes have to stay in the suitcase. All, apart from us, are Austrians. One of the bigger boys told me that Mr Hurwitz was hoping to bring the parents over as well. They can all live on the farm, that is where we are going to go on the 28th June. The holidays start here on that date. We shall have to work there. I have no chance of any training here to make something of myself. Earlier on, Mrs Hurwitz was here. She met us and asked us a few useless questions. I am so tired! From the pot into the frying pan.

26 June 1939

Well, if I have to stay here I shall go completely down the drain. Only work, dirty work. Nothing to learn. I have been to visit Miss Perilman. She is living comfortably with her sister. She, like everyone else, keeps telling us how well off we are. No one seems to realise what is happening.

Letter to Palestine

> Clifton Park Avenue
> Belfast
> late June 1939

Dear Inge,

At last I have the opportunity to write to you. I had forgotten to take your address with me. Grandmother sent it to me. I have a lot of news for you. On Thursday eight weeks ago I came home from school. When I entered Mutti said, and she was very white 'Go into the kitchen.' 'It is a house search, they are looking for foreign money' I undressed quickly and went into the parents' bedroom, where they had already turned everything over. The following had happened. In the morning, about 10 o'clock, two gentlemen came and wanted to speak to Vati. Mutti said truthfully that Vati was not there. So they said that they would come again later. As soon as they had left Mutti sent Tante Meta to our friends, to tell them that it looked as if the two men were coming to fetch Vati. Our friends could not do anything either but wait. You know, we Jews in Germany are easy sport. Mutti took the two silver candlesticks and gave them to Tante Else who happened to be there. And the last of our money she had from the shop she put into Tante Meta's suitcase. There were about 1000 Marks. Still Vati did not come back.

At 10 o'clock the people came back. When Mutti told them that Vati had not come back the 'gentlemen' made themselves at home in the sitting room, to wait for Vati. Mutti sent Tante Meta to the entrance door to warn Vati. He returned at 2.o'clock, was shocked, but refused to go away. He said to Tante Meta 'They will find me anyway.' Upstairs they started to search the flat in his presence. Gert, who had been home from school early, was there the whole time. Later on I came, as I already said. Now starts the most important part of this sad tale. If they found a piece of silver, which they considered too much, I heard one say 'You can make laws, but these people do what they want to'. When Vati tried to explain he was told to shut his mouth or they would strangle him. When they

demanded the key to Tante Meta's suitcase, my little Mutti lost her nerve. For they would ask Tante Meta whose money it was. Mutti ran to me into the bedroom and held her hands over her head. Then she ran out of the room back to where the men were and heard Tante Meta say that the money was hers. So Mutti shouted that it was hers. The men had waited for that moment. One of them said "Get dressed and come with me." He then took the money and said he was confiscating it. I will close the curtain over the rest. Both parents had to go. I really can't write any more about it or I shall go mad. The last weeks were dreadful. All the relations and friends were over-anxious. In the end I had to bring order into everything. I was happy to leave Germany, but I have landed in such a place, a hostel. There is no chance to learn anything. The people are very kind, but that does not help. The school Gert and I are going to be in, does not teach much. It is a village school. The teacher is anti-Semitic, that is all I needed. At the moment we are on holidays on a farm by the sea. I had a badly infected throat and a high fever after bathing in the sea. We were also sleeping in tents. I am a bit better now. I may be sent to a family, but not Gert. They don't take boys. The child will learn here. I won't write anymore. I feel bad tempered. The journey was wonderful. From London we travelled alone. A lady from the Committee put us on the train to Liverpool. We were met there as well and put on the ship. Dear Inge, next time more detail. I feel a bit weak. The first day up and so tired.
Many many regards, from

your cousin Edith.

> Clifton Park Ave.
> Belfast
> 24 June 1939

Dear Uncle Hans, dear Tante Trudel, dear Inge,

I was very pleased with your fat letter. First I must answer your questions, then write in detail how we came here, and what it is like. First your question, dear Inge. There is no Jewish school. We are in a hostel belonging to the Jewish Committee. I have heard that there might be a possibility in two or three years to go to Palestine. Hugo wanted to go to France and then to Australia. But he has not had his visa and is very upset. I am given a shilling a week and three stamps for three letters. Gert receives six pence and also three stamps. It rains a lot here, very seldom do we have good days, like today. Most of the time it is cold. The sun shines only two or three weeks here. Dear Uncle Hans, the address of the lawyer for my father I do not know. My father's friend, Mr Halpern, would be able to help. Tante Hertha pays for everything. I heard from Mr Halpern that someone had spoken to Mutti two weeks ago. She saw Vati at the same time.

To answer your questions: We had in Berlin a commercial traveller. We visited her sometimes. She had a sister in Northern Ireland, here in Belfast, whose nephew is the head (chairman) of the Jewish Committee. Mutti managed to interest him in us. After three or four weeks he wrote that he had vouched for us and given permission for it. During the next two months the 'dreadful' thing happened. Whereupon Hugo wrote to Mr Hurwitz and told him that our parents were in custody. Three weeks later we had the information that we could travel, and that with the next transport which was leaving eight days later. The journey was wonderful. I will tell you about it another time. In Belfast we were received by a young man, a member of the Committee. He took us by car to the hostel. Here in Belfast they have an independent (Jewish) Committee. They have taken about 50 children. Most of the children have been taken into well-to-do families. For the last arrivals a house was prepared. There is a matron, a cook to run it. Now we must stay here. The children are sent to school till they are 15 years old, then they are apprenticed to tailoring. For Gert and myself there is a guarantee till the age of 18 years. I would like to do window decoration. On an ordinary day we get up at 7 o'clock. We go to school at 8.30am. In the afternoon at 12.30 we come home, then we have lunch. At 1.30pm we go to school again. Until 3.30pm we are at school, we go home then. About 4.30pm is Cheder (religious instruction and Hebrew). At 9.30pm we have to be in bed.

During the long holidays, which we have at present, the members of the hostel have gone to the farm by the Irish Sea. We have been here for four weeks. The first three weeks we slept in tents. Now we are in a few empty rooms in the farmhouse. It is very comfortable. The food is very English. In the hostel, on the other hand, there was Austrian food. The matron and the cook stayed in the hostel. Here there is a German couple in charge. They came a few days after us. Their eldest daughter came before them. Then came the parents and three siblings. The Committee vouched for them. The Committee tries to help all the parents. But we were the last ones. So it will take a long time. Most of the parents have already got a visa. All parents will come and live on the farm. They are going to build blockhouses (?). It will be a village of 100 people. We know where our parents are, they are in the prison in Fuhlsbuttel near Hamburg. It will be months before they can leave the prison and they still have no entry visa to anywhere. You have no idea what it is like in Germany. The grandparents had to take two people into their house. Then they had to sell the house.

Every month there is another law. Following that a lot of innocent people are arrested and locked up. That is what happened to Vati. He should have run away.

26 June 1939 (continued)

The other day we made a boat trip of one hour. It was lovely. At first I felt sick, but later on I could enjoy the trip in peace. There has been no more talk about my going into a family. There is no one I can discuss it with. The people in charge are also emigrants and very egoistic. I shall have to take what is available. I am play acting so no one knows what I mean. A lot of the local people are sorry for me, when they hear what happened to my parents. None of them speak German. That does not help me. We have very few newspapers, and then only Belfast ones. I would be pleased to have a newspaper in German or English, that told us more about the world. To read in English or speak, is no problem. What will happen to us in the future I don't know. I would like to leave here. The acquaintances through whom we came are living in Belfast, but have a very small existence. Gert is well. I find it difficult to wash laundry and dishes. Every other day I am on kitchen duty. Yesterday, on Tisha Be'Av, I fasted for the first time. It went well.

We are eleven boys and five girls here. I found a good friend and Gert has two friends, who tend to lead him into trouble.

I shall always write to you, as soon as I get post from you. Inge must be able to speak perfect English, but I would prefer to correspond in German. Is Tante Trudel's mother with you yet? Who are the cousins who give Hebrew lessons to Inge?
My dear ones, many many regards, continue to love me,

Yours Edith

P.S. Gert is unable to write. He has gone out swimming. The Irish sea is two minutes from the farm. I want the letter to go quickly. Edith.

Untersuchungsgefaengnis Hamburg
Hamburg 13 August 1939.

Jacobowitz Wilhelm to children

My dear children,

After we have made a step forward, I can send you a few lines. About your letters to the relations and to Mutti and me, they gave me great joy. Tante Meta copied them and sent them to me, and I exchanged them with Mutti. That life is so good to you there is God's blessing. The trials which come our way, one has to bear, it is fate in life. Who do I turn to, to write to thank them for your visa. I am allowed once or twice a month, to write to you. Perhaps you, Edith, if you have free time during an afternoon, go to Miss Perilman and let her teach you to cut out and sewing. I shall teach you to sew. I am so glad that you are so happy there. Gert, you lazy writer, have you forgotten your parents and relations? Keep together, you depend on each other. Keep your hair cut short, as I like it and start boxing again. Be diligent in learning and behave as a gentleman. When we will see each other again, I cannot say, but the trial is in one or two months. I hope you have your winter clothes with you, if not, write to Tante Hertha. I give my regards to Mrs

Wolff and Miss Perilman. I want to thank her brother too and hope to meet him with my wife and thank him. I hope to hear from you soon and remain with love and a thousand greetings and kisses your loving father.

Hans Jacobowitz from Palestine (?) date

to Wilhelm Jacobowitz

> Untersuchungsgefaengnis Hamburg-Stadt
> Holstenglacis 3, Hamburg 36.

My dear Willy,

I often have news from your children and am glad to tell you that they are both well and happy. We are trying to get certificates for both and hope that we shall succeed. We are all well and hope you and Else are too. If it is possible, answer me to Amsterdam, Postbox 601. I would like to know when you and Else will finish your prison sentence. Perhaps Else is already free, but we don't know. Do not worry about your children, I am in constant touch with them and they are well looked after. With hearty greetings and kisses from all of us

Hans

> Refugee Farm, Millisle,
> County Down, Northern Ireland
>
> July 1939

Dear Uncle Hans, dear Aunt Trudel, dear Inge,

Many thanks for your lovely letter. You are wrong, Uncle if you think that letters are getting there, but I shall try it. To Braunsberg in Berlin I shall not write again. Two weeks ago I had a nasty letter from Hugo. He threw in my face that I was ungrateful, cheeky, full of irony and disrespectful. I see no reason to write again.

Dear Inge, you ask me about the school, but I have not been there, so I cannot tell you. At home I was never allowed to fast, But here on the farm I have gained ten pounds in weight. The food is so English, always beefsteak! Brrr...! I am very glad that you sent me newspapers. I am sorry that grandmother has been told about what happened. That means she will have no peace., and she is already so delicate. I don't believe what the papers say. They write what they want to. Most of them have no idea what is happening in reality. I cannot forget the dreadful days. This letter was left for a day. In the meantime things have changed again. Yesterday Mr Hurwitz came. I went to him and asked him to help Vati and Mutti. He listened. I shall report the talk. I: I would like to ask you something. He takes me aside. I: My aunt from Germany has written that my parents can only be freed, if they get a permit or so. Mr H: Have your parents an Affidavit or so? I: No, they have no permit or visa. Mr H: How old is your father ? I: He is 49 years old. He wanted to go then. I said: It is terrible in the German prisons. Especially for a woman. He then said that it was not possible for him to do anything at the moment, till the housing was completed. Yes, that is how it is. I shall be starting a training scheme soon. Do you know what that means ? You learn a trade and get pocket money between 5 or 7 shillings. I am not going to like it, but will start earning. Hurrah, I have just received a letter from Hugo and one of my aunts. I shall enclose them to you. Everything is changing for the best. From now on please write to us separately. Gert will stay on the farm and I am going back to town.

Many hearty regards

your Edith

Clifton Park Ave. Belfast
Northern Ireland

29 August 1939

Dear Uncle Hans,

Many thanks for the international answer stamps. I was so glad to have them and am now answering as soon as possible. I received your newspapers and am so happy with them. Most of it is interesting, but it is all so difficult. A few days ago I received documents from Woburn House (re going to Palestine). I have sent them off. Dear Uncle, this letter has stayed with me for a day. You must know how very sad the situation is. And today I received a card from Germany, from Hugo. In it he said goodbye. He wrote that there would probably be no more post and gave me addresses of other people in case I need help. From Vati I had a letter from Hamburg also to say that he could write every four weeks. Please send me both letter and card back. Ach ja, now there is nothing to be done. I hope for the best. By the time you receive this letter, everything will have been decided. Never has the writing of a letter been so difficult as today. All the time I am thinking of the good parents. Do I have to give everything away that I love? War is nothing but a small word. All the dead behind it, the death is dreadful. You can only speak of luck, if you can be together. All the time we are sitting by the radio and listen to the news, which are changing all the time. Gert is sitting beside me and keeps pestering me for chocolate. I would like his worries. But in a way that is good, and when he laughs I suddenly feel that Inge is beside me.

Many hearty greetings from your

        Edith.

Card from Hugo Braunsberg

Berlin-Gruenewald
29 August 1939.

Dear children,

Your lines have given us great pleasure, for which many thanks. I am writing to you today with special sorrow, as it may be possible that events of special danger may happen, which we dare not think about. Under those circumstances civilian letters between countries will not be possible. That would mean complete interruption for you from you and your relatives. You would be left to rely on your own, to decide all the possibilities without anyone to discuss them with you. All that, in spite of your young years, having to make decisions. I have confidence that both of you will have the seriousness and understanding which your situation will demand of you. I still believe that the future will turn out for the best, but we have to think of every eventuality. I therefore send you all my best wishes and hope that we shall see each other again in good health. Herewith the addresses of relations to whom you could turn if necessary.
I embrace you with all my heart and remain your cousin

Hugo.

Uncle Heinrich Cohen, London, NW6, 13 Wolver Lane
Tante Meta Rothenberg, London W2, 54 Kendal St.
Rosi, Paris 11, 14 Rue Greuot
Braunsberg, London EC4, 60 St. Paul's Churchyard.

Copy of BBC Talk in 1962

In July 1939 we were sent to the farm near Millisle. This had been intended for trainees, who were preparing to go to Palestine. The Jewish Committee felt there was enough room to accommodate the children for whom they had made themselves responsible. I had looked forward to living in the country, as I had really no idea what it was like. City children imagine all sorts of idyllic situations.

It rained all day, as we arrived on a sea of mud. Our dining room was an old stable, which the rain trickled into gently. The sleeping accommodation was two large tents, into which camp beds were put side by side. The ladies of the Committee party tucked us in gently with a hot water bottle, and bade us good night. Outside was a howling wind and rain as we dozed off. In the night we woke up, at least I did, to find I was soaking wet. The tent leaked. The boys' tent had packed up somewhat sooner and in the early hours of the morning all of us were huddled in wet clothes in the dining room. The following night we moved into the cow stable. This was much better as it had been whitewashed the day before. Any wet paint descending during that night was ignored, as it was warm and dry. The days were rather pleasant that July before the war, even Ireland can produce glorious weather. For a lot of us the primitive surroundings with extra work were surely a good thing. As the weeks went by, the farm became more habitable. Old buildings were patched up, and the old farm house became the centre for cultural activities. If we had not been waiting for news of our loved ones, it could have been fun. All of us lived in the hope that they would be able to leave Nazi Germany before the gates finally closed. Alas, the time ran out and on the 3rd September 1939 the war for many of us, had not just started, but become a sign of defeat. We knew that whoever had not left the continent or had had a visa stood little chance of coming out. I remember standing at the bottom of the farm house steps listening for the news bulletin. We were supposed to be in bed, but who can sleep. when they are homesick, hate the country of their birth and almost mourn for their loved ones.

After this the pendulum changed somewhat. There were those who despaired and those who started to look at the possibility of a new life. All this was interrupted when every now and then news came through a neutral country about the transporting to the concentration camp of a relative, or certain death. But the routine of life goes on. All the children under 14 years were sent to school, the ones over that age were being 'trained'. In the first attempt to strike out on my own, I looked for and found a job in Belfast. It was in the factory of my guardian. I sewed on buttons for the day, and lived again in the refugee hostel. After a while I became nanny to the grocer of the Jewish Community. He had two delightful children, whom I was supposed to look after. But it was mainly the baby who was in my charge. For the factory work I had received two shillings and six pence pocket money out of seven shillings and six pence. Five shillings went for my board and lodgings. As a nanny I received five shillings per week, from which I had to pay half to the hostel. Try as I wanted, I could not save, though I managed to give my brother a little pocket money. The Committee of the hostel complained that I was using too much shoe leather, but I assured them that I was very happy and at the same time prayed that the reason for this would not come out. I had discovered the literature of this country in a small bookcase in my employer's sitting room. This had been covered in dust when I arrived. I suppose that the books were a wedding present, to me they were a godsend and in some ways an open door. I used to perform my duties as quickly as I could and then take the baby for a walk. I was very keen on that walk in all weathers. A bottle of milk or water, as the case may be, wrapped in a clean nappy, but under my coat hidden Dickens or Thackeray. We used to go through the side streets of the neighbourhood, I always fearful that someone would spot me while I was reading. As soon as the baby made a noise, she was sucking her bottle. These walks took as long as possible, even in bad weather. As the weeks wore on, I was able to understand the language better. My English presented four years of concentrated grammar at school in Germany, and my vocabulary was, to say the least, somewhat limited.

As the summer of 1940 drew to an end, so did my occupation as a nanny. I returned to the refugee farm in Millisle. Here, time had not stood still. A long, wooden building had been erected, something like a prefab. This building gave the married couples and older members of the farm small rooms. For the younger generation there were large dormitories. The most exciting new thing was showers, though they seldom functioned to satisfaction. And instead of two boys moving the privy every two days (it needed it, there were nearly 100 people) there were flushed toilets. What bliss ! There were also two recreation rooms and a room for the synagogue. During this time the older members of the Community decided to give the children some mental exercise. So after work, classes got going. Funnily enough, if I remember right, the teaching of English was not amongst this. We had French lessons, music appreciation and continental law. I remember a test case, when I was accused of stealing certain items of underwear.

My prosecutor had been a well-known lawyer in Germany, and so I was convicted. It came as rather a shock, as I took it so seriously and felt so innocent. But then I had no sense of humour. Music was quite an item in our life. We used to hold competitions as to who could whistle a whole symphony or other such piece, without a mistake. I think 'Eine Kleine Nachtmusik' was the nearest I got. But there was no end of talent. The older inhabitants, boys and girls between 18 and 25 had begun to accept the group of children which increased their group from 40 to 80, and the additional adults, who had slowly drifted to the place, as there were many more refugees who needed somewhere to live.

Twice a week there were concerts on gramophone records. We had been given a record player and 100 records by a member of the Committee. We were also doled out the necessary clothing twice a year. At first our pocket money was one shilling per week, with three stamps. Later many of the older ones protested at this salary, and it was increased to two shillings and six pence per week. The trainees, who had formed the original party, pooled their resources, as they would have done in Palestine.

On Jewish high days and holidays great trouble was taken to celebrate the occasion properly. The recreation room sounded to the echo with the younger ones dancing the horrah, the villagers who lived half a mile away could hear it.

We did not have much contact outside the farm. As soon as the war broke out we were classed as enemy aliens. This restricted our excursions. We had to be in the grounds at 10pm and as it was difficult for transport, it was just as well to stay on the farm.

Diary   9 October 1939.

I have been on the farm three months. I have learnt a lot and made friends with two of The Chalutzot.
When we came to the farm nothing was prepared. The first night we slept in an old house, the next two weeks in tents. Soon after that I became ill, and was sent back to Belfast for four days. When I came back, we moved into the farm house.

Group at Millisle, 1943. Front row, left is Robert Sugar; Gerd is in the pale jacket. Rear centre, with glasses, is Walter Kammerling

(This letter was one of the first which I wrote in English)

To Hans Jacobowitz, Palestine   Clifton Park Ave
                                       Belfast 30 October 1939

Dear Uncle,

I thank you for your dear card. I am happy about your proper answer. I have always news from the grandparents and Aunt Meta. Hugo is in Belgium, a week ago. I am so happy about this. Only Aunt Hertha does not write any line. It seemed that my parents are well. Hugo wrote : All your relatives are alright and as I understand there is much hope to see your mother free in the near future. Gert is now alone on the farm. Next Sunday I will go and see him. He will have his birthday on the 18th November. Today a lady of our Committee went and bought me a pair of shoes.

You see, we lost all our luggage. And so we have not much to wear. I am very lonely. I had friends on the farm. Here is a very wet climate. The whole winter it is raining and terribly dark. It is also very cold, because there are no stoves, only some fire places. My work begins at 8.30am and I finish my work at 5.45pm. On Saturday and Sunday we have nothing to do. Sometimes I go to friends of my parents. I was only once in the pictures since I am here, but I was very disappointed. I would like more to go and see an opera. But there is no music here. You wrote, if it may be to come to you now. I don't think so. I would like to come to you, but I think, that it would be better to wait until the war is ended. I hope that will be soon. Now I have to finish. I hope that you will answer soon.

With many kisses

Your Edith

Clifton Park Ave
Belfast 10 November 1939.

Dear Uncle,

I thank you very much for your dear card. Gert is on the farm and I am working in Belfast. There I find a job dressmaking. Last week I started. The last time I only received letters from London and Sweden. A week ago I got a letter from grandmother. She is very unhappy, because there is no change with my parents. She is knitting a pullover for me, because she cannot do something else. My poor parents!

Aunt Meta is the only one who can go and buy. I get 7½ shillings a week. But I save most of this. I am living again in the home. It is not so nice as on the farm. In a big room eight girls sleep. It looks like a hospital. It is always cold. The whole time it is raining. My laundry is in my bags. There is no cupboard, nothing at all.

I work in the shop of the president of our Committee. He is a very nice man and helped twenty Jewish people to come to Belfast. He gave the permit for us too. I did not like very much to go to the town, because I lost friends. Now I must begin again to find somebody. I have to get up at 7.30 am. At nine o'clock I am in business. I have my Lunch at 1pm and at 6pm I have to go home. In the evening I write letters or wash my laundry. Sometimes I have to help in the kitchen. Now I have to shut the letter. Excuse my mistakes because I do not know the language very well.

With kindest regards and kisses

   Your Edith.

Dear Inge, thank you very much for your regards,
your cousin   Edith

Diary   20 November 1939   Belfast

I have been ill, very ill. Spent some time in bed. The parents are by now six months imprisoned. Gert was eleven two days ago. Last Sunday I visited him on the farm. It was wonderful. Now I must go to Mr Hurwitz again. He must help me with the parents. I am sitting in the sitting room with my friend's parents. It is good to have peace and write. Twice I have been in hospital for a blood sample. I am afraid of it. I feel so different to all the other people. Yet I am stupid. Know nothing about housekeeping or other science. It is all the fault of Ernst. Why did they not kill me when I was born. Did Mutti not realise what an unhappy being she had produced? Dear God help me. I went to work for four weeks. No one knew that I had bladder trouble. But it came out and I was told what a fool I was. I was in bed for one week. A very bad doctor came. Now I had a letter for the hospital. I went with Gans (a medical student in the hostel). He asked me a lot of questions on the way. Well, we came to the hospital. I had to get undressed. It was so embarrassing, because all the students were watching me. At first, I refused. Gans laughed at me and said: 'They are all doctors'. At first they asked me questions through an interpreter and then they examined me. I was red with shame, I could hardly stand. Then we went. On Friday I met Gans coming down the stair, and he said :'Wash yourself, we are going to the hospital tomorrow'. Who does he think he is. I started crying again the following evening. Hugo is in Belgium. Gert is well, He is growing well. He is going to be very handsome.

Diary   26 November 1939   Belfast

I am in bed again. What shall I do? I will try to help people, will try to suffer without complaining. I would love to write songs and poetry. Today I felt so very homesick. Mutti, I long for you. You are the only one who loves me without asking anything. It is so long since I had a kind word from you: 'Edithchen, my big daughter' My mother my dear little mother.

I had no luck with Hurwitz. I came home in a terrible state. What will happen when I am well again. Shall I go back to the business? Must I stay here? Or will I go back to the farm. I am so worried about it. I wrote to my friend on the farm. Shall I get up tomorrow? Why am I so weak? I shall make my bed now and try to sleep.

---

postcard to Hans Jacobowitz,   87 Keren Kayemeth Blvd.
                              Tel Aviv
                              P.O.B. 1132
Written in English   2 December 1939

Dear Uncle,

Why did you not answer? I was waiting for a card. What is the matter. And if you have no time I think that Inge can write too. Inge, you have your parents with you and you don't know what there is in living without them. Please write soon. Are you working now or are you going to school? Hugo is now in Belgium. He wrote twice to me. Inge, I am very lonely, without a friend. That is not so easy. Please answer soon.

With love Edith

Diary   3 December 1939.
        Clifton Park Road, Belfast

I am still not well. I doubt that I ever will be. I thought Gans (the medical student) would help me, but it is over. In a week it will be Chanukka. For Gert there is a knitted scarf, knitted by me, and a few bits. He will be pleased. I am just sorry that I really don't know him. What can I do now ? Everything is so difficult. I left everything behind and am looking forward to the future rather anxious, but a little trust. I don't love anyone, honest Edith? I thought I loved G, but only like Hugo, like a cousin or brother. I like my friends Putzi and Inge well. The only ones I really love are the parents. I think about the past with an easy thought. Last week I had an injection and then a blood test. Now I am studying a book, First Aid. Mutti, I think of you.

14 December 1939.

Well, time goes on and it is difficult to tell everything, in proper line. Last Wednesday I was at the hospital again, and was prescribed some medicine. Thursday one of the Chaluzoth from the farm was here. One of the members of the Committee came. He is not married and a lot of talk is about that. Yesterday I received three letters. One with the keys to the baskets, one from Hugo in English and one from the farm from Heini (David Hurst) and Rita. Gert wrote as well. On Saturday we started our festival. On Sunday Gert was here. It gave me much pleasure. In my eyes, he is most handsome and getting big. One of the Chalutzim was here. His name is Zwi. I wanted to talk to him for a minute and went into Putzi's room upstairs. We had not started to talk, when Mrs Rosenberg entered. Zwi left at once, but there was a real row. I was accused of being in a room alone with a boy. To sit in a room with a boy was immoral. I would like to know if I have no morals, of course, I have. But now it has been made into a proper 'Klatschgeschichte.'

On Monday came a card from Uncle Hans telling me that the parents are free. I don't believe it. I received a letter from James after a long time. I am longing for something, but do not know what it is. At the moment they are playing old songs on the radio. The medicine I am taking tastes foul.

Mutti, I am homesick for you. Here you never hear a kind word. Everything is pushing one around. Dear God, do help. How do you find the something that I am longing for? Shall I become more silent ? I think that would be the best. In loneliness one is bound to grow up, I have been told, yet most people are gregarious. There is no end to the war. What is going to happen I don't know. I am longing for peace. Chanukka is passed.

19 December 1939.

Yesterday I had a card from Uncle Erich (Sweden). He told me that Vati and Mutti are free at last. Now I am happy. In two weeks I shall go back to business. Our room is so dirty. But it is impossible to be angry about it.

10 January 1940.

A new year has started. Sylvester was very depressing. We all played kissing games, but I refused. At midnight I swore to keep an eye on my morality for the next year. The year started with my quarrelling with everyone around me, never mind why. Today I had a letter from Vati. The parents are still in the same place. Vati asked me to keep a diary. I answered at once. Now I must try to write each day. At the moment we only have one shilling pocket money. I have so much to get from it. Ach, Vati and Mutti, I am so homesick, and I am longing to see Gert.

---

postcard to Hans Jacobowitz, 87 Keren Kayemeth Blvd. Tel Aviv

In English 10 January 1940.

Dear Uncle Hans,

I did not get a letter a long time ago. I have to ask you very important thing. Could you help my parents? All my hopeless is on you. I can't help, but please write to all the relatives and ask them to help. My parents are not free yet. They are in the prison still yet. I got today a copied letter from my father in which he asked me to help them. I am very unhappy that I can't do anything. Please answer quickly.

With many kisses,   Your Edith.

A letter which was never sent, probably written in November 1939.

Dear good Aunt Meta,

I have been delighted to receive your beautiful letter. It came at a difficult time. I cannot describe to you how I felt. I had already been ill for eight days. In a big room with seven beds. It is bitterly cold. Now I have been up for three days. Believe me, at times I would like to end it. Just think, I am in a factory. The whole of my work consists in folding aprons, to iron, to sew on buttons, and run up and down. From the pay of 7½ shillings, I receive 2½ shillings. The rest is kept by the boss and saved for us, so he says. He is the most human of the lot here.

By and large the people here are very kind. But we are refugees and refugees again. I am, thank God, not too badly off. I have good food and drink. But for evermore I would not like to stay here. You know, so alone. Gert is very well on the farm. He has been given an almost new coat for the winter, as well as underwear and shirts. Please send the things. I need a warm dress and a pullover but especially underwear. But I would willingly do without all that, if my poor parents were to be released. Hugo wrote to the contrary I have connections to Sweden, Holland and Belgium. But there has been no answer for four weeks. You mention my being so thin. Oh, I became quite fat on the farm. My face is filling out. I gained about ten pounds in weight. You want to know what has happened to Hugo ? He wrote that he has been there (Belgium) for a few days. He will forward messages. Everything has to be in English and short. Well, that is all. No one can help me. I need a good friend, male or female, who would help me, so life would not be so helpless. I miss Mutti very much.

If you love me a little bit, you will tell no one about me. I shall have to manage.
Many thanks

Edith.

Diary   Monday 29 February 1940   Clifton Park Ave. Belfast.

It is difficult to write at times. Here in the house is a measles epidemic at the moment. Today there is the fifth case. The whole hostel is infected. My God, these doctors are bad. I went to one for a health certificate. He gave it to me at once, the incompetent. I have a good place as a nanny. Because of the measles I have to stay at home. In the kitchen this morning there was a row, because the toast was too dark. I am jealous of the other girls. I like Jurgen. A friendship is no crime. Vati wrote to behave as if he were here. Well, that is what I am doing. Simple friendships here are regarded with horror. Belfast is a narrow-minded place. The kitchen service is a torment. Naturally, everyone tries to make it more difficult. One wants tea, another milk or coffee and so on. At times I feel as if I had been on the treadmill.... There is pressure on my bladder. The usual four weekly.

Saturday evening something dreadful happened to me. I went with Putzi and Inge to the cinema, Capitol. There was quite a good film Union Pacific. By chance we were divided and I sat alone, with two empty seats beside me. A boy came and sat beside me. Suddenly I felt a hand on my thigh. For a moment I was shocked. I pushed the hand away and moved forward in my seat. I then noticed the arm on the back of my seat. I thought, I am no street girl, got up and sat down a row behind. But the enjoyment of the film was spoilt. I had to leave Germany for that. I hope to go back to work soon. I have to look after two children. Really no work, money and food. I only wish that I was back. Yesterday in the afternoon we had a big debate. One of the boys swore about his position as a refugee. One of the Committee was there and became red in the face. What is clear is, that to whine is not the answer. Manfred P. said that one had to be optimistic. That is partly true, but it is alright for him, he is studying. But for me and Gert? It does not look very rosy.¬ Friday I had a letter from Dessau over Sweden. It looks bad. Everything is getting worse. What can I do? I feel so helpless. How long will there be war? A great shame in the 20th century. Sunday, two weeks ago I was with Gert. He is looking well. A pity I have no picture of him... Now they have stopped the pocket money. Disgusting, how shall we pay for stamps ? Shall we cut them out of our ribs ?

In the evening. Is everyone crazy? Again a scene in the kitchen. Billet the cook shouts and swears at me. Everything annoys her. She does not vent her rage on those responsible, oh no, I get it in the neck. I am supposed to do everything deliberately. I am supposed to be crazy. I shall have to go and see Blumenberg, who is in charge and speak with him. No one needs to think that I will put up with this. I curse everyone who uses the situation.

Letter to Uncle Hans   Written in English   16 February 1940.

Dear Uncle,

I was glad to get your dear letter. It is terrible that no one can help my parents to come out of those circum¬stances. I can't send you the letter of Vati, but I know what he meant. I think he needs both money and a permit. I don't know how long he is condemned. But he is not free yet. I did not get letters from Hugo since November of the last year. But Gerda Cohen was together with him in Antwerp and he does not live very good. It seemed to be very hard for him.... Why does Inge not write to me. I think you begin to forget me. It. is not easy for me. I am children nurse by two little children. You will say: 'Why do you not learn anything?' Oh, I give you the answer, if you would be in my circumstances you could not learn either. I am unhappy about it, but I hope that when the war is over there could be a chance to go to one of my relations. I am lonely, please write soon.

Many regards and kisses   Your Edith

Diary   30 January 1940.   Clifton Park Ave. Belfast

This morning I was so tired that I could not get up. I slept till half ten and then got up. In the meantime Mr Blumenberg had been in the room, rather surprised at me sleeping so long. Apart from all other matters, my limbs and head are very heavy. I did not say anything about it. I helped in the dining room later with another. After washing up with Miss Levy, I played ping pong. About half five I went back to bed, where I slept till seven o'clock. Downstairs they were busy eating and listening to the radio. There was the voice of Adolf Hitler. I had my meal and asked for nothing else. It's eight o'clock and I am in bed again. Every part of me feels like lead. I would give a kingdom for a kind word. They think that I am lazy. That is what Mr Blumenberg said before he left me. I shall get up early tomorrow.

3 February 1940.

It is Saturday evening. What a crazy world. I will continue with my last happenings. On the 31st I got up early. The duty is a torment and hateful. I was well again. In the morning I had to wash our rooms. I had to lift the heavy cleaning bucket. I felt a pull and had pain on the right side. Next morning again early duty. Thank God I felt well.

Friday, that means, last night, it was miserable, always alone. No one to care for me. Today, Saturday, I was quite alone. No one was there. So I danced to the radio in the dining room and sang Hebrew songs in the Committee room. The day after tomorrow I shall go to work again.

Now something else. It's the war, the most dreadful thing to have happened. Everything is torn apart, and it is a difficult time. But when you listen to people talking, everyone thinks that if they were Chamberlain or Churchill things would have been different. I personally don't understand politics, but what the others talk about seems to be nonsense. Today it was dark at seven o'clock. What can one do tonight? Be bored with grace. Last night Miss Levy and I sat in the dining room and talked. She told me that the world was open to me. If I could do what I wanted, I would run away.

Always, I am writing a letter to you Mutti. Dear Mutti, come to me. You are my only Mutti. Take me away from all this talk. I can hear stupid Jazz on the radio. I could break it. No post from Gert. My little brother. Monday we shall have the pocket money of the last two weeks. Must finish now. It is not necessary to fill this book with sad thoughts.

6 February 1940.   My second day with the child. It is good here. No post.

11 February 1940.   It is my second week with the Leveys. So far so good.

Translation of letter from   Hans Jacobowitz
Tel Aviv 28 February 1940
87 Keren Kayemet Boulevard, P.O box 1132

Dear Edith,

Yesterday we were delighted with your first letter and your photo. We see that you put on some weight and it suits you. Unfortunately there is no news about your brother, about whose life we would like to hear. Where is he at the moment? Do you see him sometimes or are you in contact by letter? I would like to know something about this and hope that when you write next, you will give us plenty of information. You can write in German. There is no censor with post to Palestine. We still have no news from Hugo, and we are very worried about his not writing. To write again to him seems senseless. I have heard nothing from any of the other relations in Germany. Only the grandparents in Dessau sent a letter. They are still in Dessau and complain very much about the cold, which has been worse by the lack of heating materials. We have noticed nothing like that here. The lowest temperatures here are 10 degrees centigrade. As it is possible to write from here to enemy countries, I shall try to write a few lines to your father. Hopefully, he will receive them and be allowed to answer. I shall certainly let you know the result, but as long as I am uncertain about the length of his sentence, it will be too difficult to get the authorities interested in his case. As far as I know there is some money. I sent an S.O.S. to my brother in Amsterdam and asked him to help. But until now I have not had an answer. My brother will go to New York at the beginning of February, as he does not like Holland for several reasons. That Inge has not written to you, is more my fault than hers. She is not lazy and has not forgotten you. We keep our post short and to facts. There are some letters she has written that have not been sent, because there is nothing important in them. Inge has been having medical treatment in the last two months. She is having a part of her jaw rebuilt. She had the operation with good results, but she has lost two front teeth. Now she will have a metal regulator on her teeth for years, until the teeth are normal. She will be finishing business school in four months, Then I will try and find her a job. Whether I succeed is another matter.... Naturally, it would be good if you came to Palestine, although to my mind you are much better off where you are, than most children here. There are very many children here and a job like yours is not possible here. Apart from everything else, this country is very poor and there is not much money for refugees. In England or Ireland that is quite different, but I will try to approach the officials of the Youth Aliya. A few days ago for the first time, twelve children from England arrived since the outbreak of war. Perhaps you could write a few lines to the Jewish Agency in London, best of all to a Mr Feuchtwanger, who is working there. I think the address is Great Russell Street. Then you will be able to judge for yourself. Tell the people the situation, that of your parents, and that you have no relatives in the British Isles, although there are a few relations here. Try, of course, to include Gert, because your parents would not like it if you were separated. You do not have to write a lot, but to the point. You can write in German, as Mr Feuchtwanger came away like you. His address is as far as I know: c/o Jewish Agency for Palestine, Great Russell Street, London. Well, try your luck with that. I have heard nothing from Tante Hertha. We don't even know where she is. Unfortunately you give no information about the family you are working for? Are they religious alike (Glaubensgenossen) and how old are the children? About the length of the war one cannot talk unfortunately. It appears to be a hard struggle and could last a few years. It is all in the stars and we don't know what fate has in store for us. Are you still in the hostel or with the family? Are you educating yourself in English or do you just absorb what you hear in the course of the day?

We would be very happy to have a few lines from you, in which you answer all the questions that I have asked you today. Let me know what the Jewish Agency answers. And if you meet a lady from WIZO (Women International Zionist Organisation), ask her if they cannot fulfil your wishes.

Give greetings to your brother from us all,
Regards and kisses to you from us all.
Your loving Uncle Hans

Letter from Hans Jacobowitz to Wilhelm Jacobowitz,
Untersuchungsgefaengnis
Hamburg Stadt Holstenglacis,
Hamburg 36.

My dear Willy,

I often have news from your children and am glad to tell you that they are both happy and well. We are trying to get certificates for both and hope that we shall have success. We are all well and hope you and Else are as well? If possible, please answer me to Amsterdam, Postbox 601. I would like to know when you and Else will finish your punishment. Perhaps Else is free already and we do not know ? Don't worry about your children. I am in constant touch with them and they are in good care.
With heartiest greetings and kisses from us all,
Your Hans

Letter from my mother to Hugo, already in Belgium. The date is wrong by one year. No doubt this letter and all that followed were written under great stress.

Berlin, 8 March 1939 (?)

Dear Hugo,

At last I can write to you directly. A very hard time is behind me, but with greatest of good fortune my husband was released on the

same day, for we have been free since the 6th March. Now we are living for the time being with your dear mother and are feeling very happy. On Sunday we shall visit the Old ones in Dessau. I thank you so very much for all you did for our children and are still doing. For it is very difficult for you. I am asking you to send the enclosed letter to Edith. The children will certainly be very pleased to have this news.
With very best regards,
I am your dear aunt
Else

Edith's cousin, Hugo Braunsberg

Taken in 1935

Berlin, 17 March 1940

My dear Hugo,

Many thanks for your quick reply to my news. Yes, you are right, my husband and I, in spite of everything never lost our courage, and we are convinced that somewhere there will be a country where we can be together with our children and can earn a crust of bread.

We have been to all the necessary offices to put our name down with as much urgency as possible; but as you know with all the difficulties, everything is so difficult and in the end falls apart. Our friends put our name down for 'Apalea' and we have been asked to get a medical certificate. But it is a question of money. ... The affair in Hamburg is all over, thank God. There was a great trial, which lasted three days. We were on the periphery, and had nothing to do with the main trial. I was pardoned completely, as I had stated from the beginning that I had done nothing. So I was in prison for ten months unnecessarily.

My husband received a punishment considered as having been served by his time in prison. Half an hour after the trial we were free. They have not released my money. But I am so happy that we are both free, that this seems unimportant.

The reunion with the grandparents was also very touching. It is very sad that one can see how the body and mental strengths deteriorates in people who one loves. Both of them, grandfather and grandmother, are only a shadow. Grandmother is intellectually very much alert, but during the time we have not seen her, her body has shrunk. She grieved so much about my sentence, that I reproach myself bitterly, to have given her so much grief. But it really was not my fault, that it happened like this. Regarding the children, I am so pleased that they are away, outside, and that they are healthy. All the same, I would have liked Edith at school, learning a trade. She did not answer to my question, why she had left the Hurwitz place. In any case, it is touching that she does what her strength permits. About the boy next time. Stay well, dear Hugochen, and receive my heartiest greetings and kisses from your dear aunt Else.

Dear Hugo, please send enclosed letter to Edith,   Else.

My dear Hugo,   29 March 1940

After your last letter, we immediately got in touch with H.V. but received a negative answer at once. We were told that there was no reason to write, and that these people only arranged travel if one

had somewhere to go. The only thing possible at the moment is Shanghai, and that needs 400 dollars per person. That is returned later on. So that is the answer we had from H.V. We are trying of course in other ways. I am starting lessons in sewing and my husband in decorating and billboard writing. We have only to pay a reasonable amount for the lessons, as we have registered at the Juedische Gemeinde for the lessons. Now, my dear Hugo stay healthy, send us some news.
Many greetings and kisses
from your loving aunt   Else

Diary

24 February 1940

It has been raining so much that it was impossible to go out. So I stayed at home all day and played with the child. The next morning when I arrived early, the child did not want to go out with me and screamed and cried. In the end the mother took both of us to the shop. At lunchtime the father drove us home. I went to the pictures on the same day. The following day, Friday, I stayed at home and watched cake making. Miss Levey showed me how to do it. After lunch I was free. I spent part of it talking to one of the students and going to the library. The evening was boring. On Saturday I was a visitor at Mrs Levey's mother. In the evening, on the stairs, I met one of the boys, who asked me why I was behaving in such a peculiar way? No post in the last three weeks. Then from Gerda Cohen and Uncle Hans. One of my letters was returned. I am homesick.

3 March 1940

A lot has happened. I wanted to go out last night but had to stay at home. All the girls had to rub their heads with petrol and wash them. Senta sat there all the time and played cards, of course she does not live here. Juergen stood behind her and gave advice. He seems to be infatuated with her. I called her into the bathroom and asked her if she liked him. She said 'no' and gave me her word. I had to go to bed, but was restless sitting on it. I left the room several times. Juergen stayed downstairs till she went and I heard him or someone else call out 'Come again soon'. I felt very miserable in bed and cried. Miss Levey and I had another chat about J. and came to the conclusion that he was a 'ladies' man.' Senta flirts and all the boys are after her. From one thing to another. It is nearly Pessach. They want to close the hostel and send everyone to the farm. I don't trust them, the holidays are going to be very long. Many here have invitations. I wanted to discuss this today with my Lady. She said that she would leave it to the Committee. So there we are. I must talk to Mrs Woolf about this.

13 March 1940

I have managed not to write anything for ten days, and today it is already 11.30 pm. and I don't know how long I can write. At work everything is going well. The only interesting things happen in my private life. I have got over my disappointment with Juergen. And he noticed it when we went home after the club on Saturday. I was very cool. I get on well with Senta. She tells me everything. She has to work very hard. This morning I had a letter from Gert. He is very unhappy and wants to be with me. I answered at once, I would like to see him too. Juergen received his labour permit today. I had a letter from Uncle Hans. That is all.

14 March 1940

I have been invited to the Leveys for Pessach. I hope the Committee will permit it. You never know with them. Purim we shall make a party here. A bit of dancing and so on. I am very sensible in how much I depend on the people here.

18 March 1940

I am so tired that my eyes are nearly closing. There was such a lot to do as the maid of the household was in Dublin. So we were alone with the children. So I was late back at the hostel and they all asked where I had been. Nobody believed me when I told them, you could see it on their faces. Does not matter. This afternoon I went for a walk with Senta. I told her a bit of gossip about the hostel. She seemed so interested in that. You have to give people what they want if you want to get on with them. Good night. I hope I shall sleep well.

27 March 1940

Madi left the hospital on Tuesday and we have started to prepare for Purim. We want to dance a Horrah and a Waltz. We rehearsed every night and I fell into bed with fatigue. I stayed at home on Saturday. In the morning we had the last rehearsal. The evening started with wonderful food. It consisted of herring salad and Haman Taschen and coffee. About six o'clock the visitors came. The first one was Mrs Woolf's son, Willi. Then came Miss Perilman and her sister. We had taken all the tables from the dining room and had put rows of chairs in their place. And at half eight it started. The choir, and that included me, sang 'Lo mir allan in ejnen' and 'Chag Purim.' After that there were recitals. To end the first part we danced the Horrah. Because of the bad piano playing it did not go right. After that we had an 'Eispause'. The second part started with the choir. The songs were 'Suntig Bulbe' and 'Moshiach wird kommen'. During the second part Mr Hurwitz and the Rabbi were present. We then danced the Waltz, it went well. Mr Hurwitz said that I looked better as a boy than a girl. I felt very pleased. The whole evening Juergen sat with Senta. But I don't care anymore, though it is difficult at times. On Monday I was the only one who had to go to work. I started on my monthly Sunday night and was very uncomfortable. This was the first time since I arrived in Ireland. Gert is well.

Letter from Gert to Dr. Feilchenfeld in New York. He forwarded letters till the USA came into the war. He was a friend of Vati's from the 'Bund Juedischer Frontsoldaten'

This was written in English.

Dear Mr Feilchenfeld, I was very glad to have news from you. I am very well. I am sleeping in a very nice room. I have it with a few

other boys. It is very warm because of the central heating. Each of us has his own cupboard. Edith room is smaller than mine. We have lots of friends. We are often invited by them. Last week there was a big Purim party. I was a little girl with blond plaits. Edith was a very nice sailor with brown cheeks and a brown mustache. I have got a new suit and a pair of shoes. I have a showerbath every evening before I go to bed. I am making a serviette holder. That is all for the day. I am going to play football.
Many regards
Your Gert

Diary

1 April 1940

Today is the first of April.

I had post on Thursday, both times from Mutti but not even regards from her. One letter to Miss Perilman, the other to Gert. I feel upset. Hugo wrote a short note, which he included with the letters. Friday in eight days it is Mutti's birthday. I shall have to write. Hugo wrote that they are worried about me. We have started dance evenings here. I am getting quite good. Earlier on I had to wash my laundry. It is so tiring. I have heard nothing from Gert. Everything is going well at work.

8 April 1940

I am waiting for post again. I am worried. (At work) We are very busy with the cleaning. It is not till Pessach. I shall stay here for Pessach, even sleep here. Yesterday, Sunday, she invited Gert for a day. How very kind. I visited Mrs Woolf and had an evening meal. She is very kind to me lately. I help a lot. Juergen and Senta are still going out, but he still won't leave me alone. My friend Madi said to him tonight: Edith does not need a Bel-Ami like you. She is far too decent. That really made the point. Madi is a good friend.

3 April 1940
62 Clifton Park Ave. Belfast

Dear Uncle Hans,

Please excuse me for keeping you waiting so long. I already had a letter ready, but since then there was post and everything became out of date.

You will know by now that the parents are free. Mutti has been writing, Vati not at all so far. It is really time to start with something. For both of them must get out. Mutti wrote with such urgency. Uncle Hans, please you must help. Under the circumstances, Gert and I are well off. I have been lucky with my work. The people are very kind to me. My main job is looking after a small baby of seven months. I enjoy that very much and feel so well. Gert is still on the farm. So far I have not written to the addresses. Time enough when the parents are here. If they go somewhere else in the end we may not be with them. Please, try your hardest. The grandparents wrote to me that it is very cold there. Here, with the bad heating it is cold as well. The fireplaces are only warm, if you stand in front of them. Otherwise it is cold. No double glazing, so there is a lot of draught.

Today I saw two double rainbows. It gave me great pleasure. I stood in the rain and looked at them in wonder. I never dreamt to see such a thing in Belfast.

I hope Inge is better by now. What bad luck (with her teeth). Thank God we are well. That is the last thing for us to get sick. The people I am working for are Jewish, of course. I would not be allowed to work for any other. Gert is on the farm. He is at a village school. I doubt that they teach him anything. He is very naughty. Apart from that he is very handsome and not bad. He needs a strong hand, but it is not there. What can I do ? We had a lovely Purim festival. I took part. Danced a Horrah and a Waltz. We have started to have dance evenings, it is fun. Can no one get an affidavit for the parents? Can Uncle Lutz help? I must close now. Please write to Tante Hertha or

the grandparents, as we have no home address, having lost our home.
Many greetings and kisses,
from your Edith

Diary

21 April 1940

This is my first long day with the Leveys. At the moment I am waiting for Gert. Fourteen days since my last entry. Life changes .all the time. I have started to be friendly with P. He is a nice boy. A hard worker and nice. I had a letter from Mutti. She wrote so sweet, I was so very happy. Gert is invited for Pessach. Solomon (member of the Committee) is giving him a lift.

30 April 1940

Yes, now the days of Pessach are over. I had my brother with me for ten days, after two months. I am returning to the hostel tomorrow, and he returns to the farm. What happy memories we shall have. I had that letter from Mutti, what a brave one. But they are all so courageous, but I feel so helpless. One has no hope to see them again. The only help would come from outside. I feel so lonely. Later on I shall eat the first piece of bread for eight days. On the radio there is modern music. We had two Seder evenings and Gert was so shy. But on the second evening we were a bit drunk. I laughed a lot. The Leveys were amused. Vera (the eldest girl) was there as well. She did not want to go to bed. A real child. Gert played with her all the time. We went to the pictures three times.

18 May 1940

I am sitting at home. I have no permit and therefore cannot work. And I only take the children for walks? And if I don't get the permit I shall have to go back to the farm.... That would not be bad during the war. In the meantime Hitler has swallowed Denmark, Norway, Holland, Belgium and Luxembourg. As nothing seems to stop him, it could be possible that we too will have enemy aircraft. That is a pleasant (?) possibility. One can imagine the feelings. In England everyone is interned. Here life is not bad. But now there is no post from home. What shall I do? I have heard nothing from Hugo. I am longing for him and would not be a bit surprised if he arrived here one day. Last week I went to the Opera twice. Once to Traviata and then to Cavalleria Rusticana. The first one was very good, the second one passable. One can't ask much here. I am going to the farm tomorrow to unpack Gert's winter clothes.

2 June 1940.

I am still at home waiting for my permit. I am helping in the hostel.

15 June 1940

I have had news from the parents and Aunt Meta. To bring things up to date: Italy is now in the war, Belgium and Holland are overrun. It is true that I do not understand much. I am so sorry for the innocent people. I am so fed up with it all. I am thinking of going back to the farm. It is unlikely that I shall get the permit. I am losing weight. All my clothes are loose. No wonder, no butter or eggs. I know that it can't be helped. The food we have does not agree with me. I have difficulty with the older girls, as I am the youngest. They pick on me. Edith here, Edith there. We have just had Shavuoth. Madi and I went to the pictures. The cinema is getting on my nerves. But one must have something to dream about. The endings are usually happy. Dreams are good, the present is so ugly. No use looking ahead. Best to sit and read books. I wish one of them were here: like Vati, Mutti, Aunt Meta, Hugo or James. Instead of that.....

27 June 1940   Millisle

Today, a year ago, I arrived in Belfast. A lot has changed during that time, but it has been told on other pages.   I received my permit. On Sunday was my first day of work. Everything went well. In the evening as I was given my tea, at the same time, she told me that she only took me back to work because she felt sorry for me. She expects me to tell her everything that is happening during the day at home. That means, carrying tales. Now, there is nothing that I hate so much as telling tales. So I thought about it and came to the decision that it would be better to be near Gert. So I gave in my notice on Monday, in spite of her protests. So now it is Thursday and I have been on the farm since Monday. Madi is here as well and that makes it more pleasant. A lot has changed here. There are many friends here, that has its for and against. All of them are so busy with the children and are trying to do well. The children are really not very easy. . . . It is lovely here. One could easily forget the outside world. The only thing to remind me of the outside is the eight o'clock curfew.

I had an interesting experience. Madi, Alec and I travelled in the company of a Dr Schayer. He told me that they had decided to make me responsible for the children. I felt quite ill. I am so nervous at the moment that I would have no patience with the children. He told me on the way that he considered me trustworthy. When I arrived on the farm so many people wanted to talk to me that I felt quite giddy. Mr Nachman complained about Gert, Mrs Schayer asked for help and Mrs Kohner talked right into me. On the first day I did not work. The last two days Madi, Alec and I have been working in the fields singling out carrots. The back and thighs feel as if they were broken. Today at four o'clock Madi and I lay down in the meadow.

28 July 1940   Millisle

I have not written for a long time. That does not mean there is nothing to write. Today is Sunday and there are so many visitors. To the devil with all these people. They want to know everything. It's like a Zoo. I must go back into the house, it's getting dark.

2 August 1940

Dr and Mrs Schayer are here to educate us. Their son came also. But only for the holidays... He is very intelligent and good to talk to. I have been buying sweets for Gert and myself, also an egg. I would give years of my life to have Mutti here. I have started to write a play. I spend all my spare time writing.

14 August 1940

I am in bed. It was fast day yesterday and it did not agree with me. Our lessons are very good. They may be useful later on. I have a pile of books beside me, but don't feel like reading. I am disappointed with the fast day yesterday. I had hoped to be spiritually impressed.

21 August 1940

Again I am alone evening after evening. I have made up my mind to use every opportunity to learn something. Juergen was here for fourteen days. He behaved badly. Today he left, thank goodness. Last evening I wrote a letter to Inge E. I sent it with someone. I was stupid last week in disclosing some of my thoughts, sharing them with other people. Now one of them is circulating what an egoist I am. Am I? I do not know. I have no peace. In another month I shall be sixteen. Already the second birthday from home. I am sure Mutti and Vati will remember. Gert has given me much pleasure the last few days. He was given one shilling and six pence for good behaviour. And he saved it for me, for my birthday. He has a little girlfriend. He seems to like them blond. Her name is Sonja. She is as blond as the other Inge from his class. Sometimes he buys them chocolate. I like it, he will be like Vati. But I don't like his friendship with M.E. This boy is such a smoothy, that he seems false all the way. And so dirty. Gert and I have little contact. During the week he goes to school and I am working. I don't even have time on a Sunday. Earlier on I went for a walk with Heini Hirsch. We talked about his favourite subject, Madi. Madi manages to turn the heads of so many boys. She also has a lot of girls as friends. Now goodbye for today. I am unable to see.

28 August 1940

Today in twenty days I shall be sixteen. Yesterday I already received my pass and another document. Gert stayed in bed today.

Fortunately nothing much. I talked to one of the others. He said that I must try and conform with the others, at least to all intent. I must try. I should try and stop making comments all the time. Dr Schayer is leaving, I am sorry for that.

During the four months of his stay here, I have learnt a lot. As a farewell gift, I received a History of Art. And he wrote in it something like this: To my dear little friend Edith Jacobowitz, I hope that I was able during the weeks of my stay here to awaken some strength into your way of a future life, and to help to strengthen your character. (I still have the book) I was so pleased to receive the gift. The book is wonderful, in 1990.

Saturday evening I felt so embarrassed. I was sitting on the wall outside the farm near the sea and Franz came along to tell me that it was forbidden. I had felt pretty depressed before and now I started to cry. It was the one thing I had promised myself was not to happen. And now I cannot look him in the face. Another mistake. Madi is going away on Sunday, so is Miss Reh. What a pity as we are in the middle of a French course. The English lessons have stopped as well. The number of people here is increasing. I feel that I have to write, write and write. As all pales with the sorrow about the parents, it is all sorrow. No one cares about us. I will and must learn something. But there is no rest. I am covered with spots, What else shall I write? About my discontent? In a quarter of an hour the light will be turned out. I have not been so late for a long time.

15 September 1940

Tomorrow I have a birthday. I shall be altogether sixteen years old. I am sitting in the radio room and am listening to the Gipsy Baron. I feel much easier today. I discussed the affairs of my heart with Mrs Letzter. She gave me good advice. If I listen to her, something should come of it. But one has to fight, fight, fight.

17 September 1940

It was the most bitter birthday ever; but Gert was very sweet.. -- -- - he gave me a fountain pen and a rain hat. Otherwise there was chocolate. How thoughtless people are. I would have preferred flowers. I am so very homesick and would like to cry like a little child. Dear God, give me strength and courage. If I only had someone.

26 October 1940

There has been an air raid warning. The children went crazy, took their coats, boots and gasmasks to bed. We will have to practise, now we know what can happen.

In the last few days I have been dancing the Horrah. But it does not agree with me. Thursday I fell over. From the parents there was indirect news. That made the religious holidays much better. I wrote a letter regarding pocket money. Much good may it do.

10 November 1940

Today two years ago von Rath was killed. Today two years ago everything was taken from the German Jews. Today two years ago we sat by the radio and listened to Goebbels. We had to pay money and we had none left. The shop had to be closed. Altogether the beginning of our end. Many of us here are fasting. Not me, as I was on duty for the Shabbath with Pinchas. I had a bad head. Through the Red Cross I received three letters from the parents..

In one of them Vati is begging for 60 dollars. I am to go to Hurwitz. Vati needs it for the journey to Shanghai. I must try and get the money. Even if I have to sell myself. 60 Dollars is a lot of money. I am so unhappy. Last night I spoke to Meir about it. He agrees that I have to do everything that is possible. I have been reading a book about Friedeman Bach.

23 November 1940

Gert's birthday has passed and I am not feeling well. Went to bed after supper last night. Last week on Thursday there was a terrific storm. It lifted the roof off the radio room and the wooden structure groaned as if the whole of it would collapse. I am working in the sewing room with all the tittle tattle. They said nasty things about my friend Inge.

14 December 1940

What shall I write about. Better do it systematically. On Monday I went for the first time to Donaghadee to the technical school. We had a sewing lesson. I started with a set of underwear. The Committee is paying for the lessons but not for the materials. I shall resew my clothes. On Tuesday we cooked something for tea. Not bad for a beginner. Next time it will be more difficult. On Wednesday there was First Aid, very boring. I nearly went to sleep. On Thursday I went to the cinema: Balalaika. Yesterday I wrote a letter to Sweden and to the Red Cross. Today I made two bookmarks for Channuka.

20 January 1941

It is nearly a month since I wrote anything. I must try and recap. Channuka is passed and we have had lovely evenings. On one of them the children performed scenes from 'Emil and the Detectives,' on another they had scenes from 'Jacob's Dream.' They performed reasonably well. I have also been to Belfast. First I went to the hairdresser and had my hair cut for the first time in a year and a half. It is looking much better now. Then I went to Mrs Woolf and Miss Perilman to sleep.

29 January 1941

Always when I want to write there are other things to do. Dreadful! Monday: sewing. Tuesday: baking. Wednesday: First Aid. I also want to mention the result of my journey to Belfast. I have got a place with Hurwitz near his office. Geoffrey, his son was very kind and thought I was sure to get a permit. Now I must wait. — — — Tomorrow there is a wedding here. The fortunate one who is on duty is of course me. Well, it can't be helped. I shall make up for it with the food. There will be chicken and cake amongst other things. I am so irritated. It's lovely living here if you are a Chalutz, but I can see that that is impossible for me. So there is this big gap between us which nothing can bridge. When Rita was still here it was not so noticeable, on the contrary.

I have got over my latest passion. It is difficult when one is so intense, but later on one understands that it is better when things do not turn out as one expects. Gert is well. He is growing into a pleasant teenager. Here on the farm there is nothing new.

2 February 1941

I am in such a state. No sign of a working permit. And I am so homesick, that I cannot sleep. It has been a terrible week. Everything is so difficult. We are expecting an invasion. But you have to leave it to the English, they are cool and courageous. I had post from Feilchenfeld and the parents. James writes every second week. He is well. He is driving tractors. Tomorrow is Sunday again. So the week starts again with all the trouble. I am starting to look at my summer clothes. In the summer I doubt that I will have time for it. – – – The wedding was very nice. On Saturday afternoon I went to bed. Some of my friends have been very unkind. That is all.

11 February 1941

I am in bed in one of the single rooms with an inflamed bladder. It really is a nasty one.

12 February 1941

For the second day I am in bed again. I have had a dreadful night. During the day one cannot sleep. First of all, the walls are so thin that you can hear people knock on doors at the end of the corridor, and otherwise I feel such an upheaval. There is nothing of importance new. I do hope I get my working permit soon. Such a bore, the waiting. Gert is well, the picture taken lately shows this. He has grown since the three months since it was taken. I find that the picture of me, makes me look very old. I read a lot, but would like to write something. But one cannot force such a thing. Last week was dreadful, as I quarrelled with everyone. Of course, today

I cannot get to my sewing lesson in Donaghadee, neither to my cooking lesson tomorrow.

At last I went to sleep. Until mealtime, when Gert came to wake me up. I feel much better now. No comparison to yesterday. I had visits from Meir, Aber and Mausche. It's nice of them (the Chalutzim) to come and see me. Pinchas came too and the others went away quickly when they saw him. It is a quarter to nine, and I am waiting for Mrs Kohner. She is supposed to have spoken to the Committee about me yesterday. That sounds interesting.

Last evening, that is early this morning, there were planes over us. I hope I shall never have to use my First Aid. If I were religious, I would pray to God. Unfortunately that is not so, which means that I have no spiritual support. Does not matter, though I wish that someone would help me with work, even with thinking and work. But it does not seem likely. If Mutti were here I would be a different person. I think, that I would not even need this book, which must surely be a sign of my loneliness.

During this Shabbath I was dreaming, that I was back home. I met all the relations, and came to..... unhappily on the Gorman's farm in Millisle. So that is life. I know that even if I find work I shall still not be satisfied. Even if I earn more than the pocket money we get. But man has to try, as my teacher of religion said: 'Every human being has the good in him and must strive to grow. To be honest, I have judged people and life by that concept. Funnily enough, I have learned that human beings are bad, they have more bad than good in them. They try to achieve in crooked ways what could be done straight forward as well. The few good ones are in a minority. But the world depends on them. The masses, by that I mean most people, who are unable to think for themselves, are just carried along. They are therefore not responsible for their badness, as they are too stupid. If one is a good puppet manipulator, one can make them dance till one laughs. They are in effect not so evil. If you control the masses, anything can be done. I despise people in the mass, and those who play with them. I never want to be influenced that way, so that I disgust myself. It's funny, I know that I have many faults, and if I don't correct them I shall be disgusted with myself. That self-consciousness must never be shown to the world at large. There is always the fear of being exposed. I spend days at times crying inside me, lacking the ability to change anything. As I write this down, it feels better. I am honest with myself, why should I lie? I should tear all this out of the book. To be honest, I cannot imagine a normal life any more. I feel, that it was unreal to have lived in a home with the parents.

7 March 1941

I don't seem to have any time to write any more. I have been busy.

22 April 1941

Pessach (Easter) is over. We all shall remember it. There was a dreadful air raid on Belfast. Many houses were blown up and windows were shattered. Here, we heard only little of it. As I came out of the door I could hear planes above me. There must have been a lot. The motors sounded familiar. They reminded me of Dessau, during my stay with the grandparents. There I heard all night the noise of planes from the Junker factory. But I went to the dormitory and to bed. Just in case, I put my track suit on my bed. As soon as I had put on my pyjamas, we could hear the first anti-aircraft guns. The wooden hut of our dormitory was shaking. Everyone jumped out of bed shouting. I put on my track suit and quietened the smaller children. I then pulled myself together and went to sleep.

5 May 1941

Our baskets arrived with our clothes after all this time. I had post from America. Oma Tinka, Vati's mother has died. The grandparents are getting weaker. Grandfather's mental state is bad. Tante Meta is working from seven to four each day. James too is worried from his letter.

6 May 1941

Last night another air attack. At the moment I am listening to the Kreuzersonate. Today I wrote to America. I wrote to Vati and Mutti that I had a boyfriend and his name was Fred. I am writing, so to make them believe that I am not taking anything serious. Feilchenfeld thinks so too. No one must know what life is like.

26 June 1941   (actual date was 22 June)

Today Germany and Russia declared war. Everyone here is full with joy. They do not think what it means. There will be blood, blood and more blood shed. My God, all is crazy. It all amounts to greed, money. I feel so lonely during this time. I have been told a lot today about fascism, communism and socialism. It made it a lot clearer. I am conscious today that the possibility of seeing my parents again is hopeless. These days there are no miracles. The only consolation is that they know us safe, and we know that they have that consolation. I think I must try to become a nurse in a hospital. I hope it is possible. Yesterday I was on a Red Cross parade. Lady Londonderry took the parade. Strangely, she had tattooed legs. Perhaps that is now the fashion with people of quality in England. All this took place in the castle of Berrisford. The master of the house, who is a confirmed anti-Semite, was as nice as sugar. We were photographed twice and the picture will be in the newspaper. Then we marched, if you can call it that, and Red Cross certificates were distributed. Mrs Kohner had her Red Cross. After that, elegant tea was served, and then we went through the garden. It is like a fairy tale, so beautiful. I could cry. On Wednesday I shall speak to the one in charge of the Red Cross and ask her if she could help me to get into a hospital. From tomorrow I am working in the Dairy, making butter, cheese and buttermilk.

27 June 1941

My second day in the Dairy. It's lovely. I have to work on Sunday afternoon, but I don't mind that because the visitors are such a nuisance. I have been reading in the paper that parts of Berlin are destroyed. It has upset me a lot. I shall move into another room so I can sleep early, being in the Dairy. I have written to four hospitals and have had one refusal. Three letters went to England and one to Belfast. Mrs Kohner and I have ordered the Nursing Times. I have also written to Mrs Berwitz, Committee, for money for a winter coat.

2 August 1941

Today I had a Red Cross letter from home. This was the content: 'My dear boy, thank you for your news. Learn to be diligent. We are healthy, but let us hear from you. Heartiest kisses, Parents.'

Vati signed it. It was dated 27 April this year.

The letter came from Erdener Strasse. A bit of light. It was a fast day yesterday, but I did not fast, as I had to work making butter. I was so tired in the evening that I went to bed early. The girl with me, Helga, has boys staying with her till 12 at night. So today there was a row. There is a certain amount of jealousy as we have such a comfortable place. I am grown up. I have a real boyfriend. And he kissed me on my birthday. My first kiss.

10 November 1941

Today three years ago everything happened. Oh, my poor parents, what you must feel today. We had a simple service to remember the pogrom. Patriasz gave a talk, Hedy read a poem called: Buchenwald. A letter from a relation was read and then we had a choir.

18 January 1942

Days pass and there are no more letters. Dear Mutti, I am a big girl. I try to dress well and look after myself. My boyfriend has other girls. He tells me that no girl goes into marriage a virgin. But I don't suppose he would marry one that is not. Not that I would want to marry an inexperienced man. Mutti, don't be shocked. Perhaps my way of living in the future might not meet with your approval. Anyway, I hope soon to get into a hospital.

Edith in 1943, aged 19

1990

I started at the Ards District Hospital in September 1942. It is not given to everyone to write in a diary 50 years old. But that is what I am doing. To sum the little diary up:
A disturbed and vain little girl, in shock most of the time, never coming to terms with what she considers and probably in fact is, a very inferior situation. A few years older, she might have made real mistakes. As it was, she was too frightened. Nothing in the book speaks of the care which was still emanating from her mother and Hugo. The latter could surely have saved himself, if we, Gert and Edith, had not held him up! Forgive us for our selfishness...

Red Cross letter from　　　　　　　　　Else Sara Jacobovitz,
　　　　　　　　　　　　　　　　　　　　　　Sybel Strasse 66,
　　　　　　　　　　　　　　　　　　　　Berlin Charlottenburg

To her brother in law:　　　　　　　　　Hans Jacobowitz,
　　　　　　　　　　　　　　　　　　　　　　　　P.O.B. 1132
　　　　　　　　　　　　　　　　　　　　　　Tel Aviv, Palestine

Dear Hans,
I am alone now. Since May 42 without Willy. Father died May 41, Mother December 42. Meta, Hertha gone.
Heartiest greetings
Trudel, Inge, Else

---

20 January 1943　　　　Else Sara Jacobowitz

Answer

Dear Else, deeply touched, always thinking of you. Edith, Gert. Nothing for long time from (my) mother, Luz (brother).

Mother blind. Keep in touch.

All my heart　　　　　Hans

---

3 May 1943

A letter from U.S.A. to my parents, probably with letters from us

Dear family Jacobowitz,　　　　　　　　　　　　　18 April 1941

There have been two letters from Edith. She is again on the Millisle farm. She has a pretty room with a seven year old boy. She has to look after him. She also has to look after the two daughters of the manager of the people there and take them for a walk. At the moment she is working in the sewing room. There she has to mend socks and trousers for the boys. I don't know if they are knitting or sewing there. They seem to iron underwear. Gert has a garden where he grows flowers and cabbages. Edith is writing pleasant letters with passable English, but she is still too childish to extract the real things. Whether there is a possibility to be trained, I cannot make out. How Gert is doing at school is also not very clear. She keeps writing about Purim and Pessach and they seem to go to the pictures and the opera, which Edith likes very much. How are Rosi and Inge ? How are things with you and your work? I hope to hear from you soon and to be able to give you some more definite news. I have asked specific questions and hope to be clearer.

Many regards,
    Yours Harry Feilchenfeld.

Letter from me (via Palestine?)   1941 (?)

Dear Uncle Willy and Aunt Else,

I was very happy with your news. It is wonderful to receive post. My brother and I are well. We often think of you and talk about you. You would be surprised how big we are now. I am so tall, that half my clothes are too small. I am still on the farm and will not leave here for some time. As far as my parents are concerned, they are supposed to be well. I was sorry to hear that Oma (my father's mother) has died. How is Aunt Meta? Is she still with Uncle Herman and Aunt Emma? (my grandparents). Your nephew James is well. He asked me to send regards. I have learned to bake. And I am glad that I can sew. So I can change and mend a shirt for Gert. We do get quite a bit of pocket money. Yesterday I sunbathed for the first time. There is lots of company and that is good. One of them is a young man with blue eyes and blond hair. Fred is very clever and we learn together. Gert is very jealous, but Fred plays with him. We get many books from the library. I read a lot in my spare time. My room has improved a lot since I put copies of

famous paintings on the wall. But the main picture is one of my parents. Gert has no time to write, as he is having Barmitzwa lessons.
Many regards to Aunt Hertha, Meta, Emma and to you
Your niece   Edith.

This letter told little of the truth, but at the time I felt that this sort of news would make them feel easy about us.

These are translations of the only letters of my maternal grandmother, Emma Gutman, which survived. They were written in 1941 from Dessau to Berlin to my mother Else, but so camouflaged, so to send them out of Germany.

Dessau May 1941

My dear children,

The news of your children seem to me like a miracle from God, and we must be so grateful for such human kindness. Everything else pales into silence and the courage increases, for work. I would like to know how many people moved in with you; if they are a family or single persons. Have they the use of the kitchen, etc? I can visualise your excitement, but perhaps it is for the best. How much would I like to help you. I hope that you will be here for Whitsun, together everything is much easier. After all the upsets, I am having a good day today and I am grateful for it. Meta sends her best regards. She knows your need for the aprons and the 'Leuchter'. Today there came news from the Tax Office; each day brings sorrow, and it needs a lot of writing and thought. Please, dear Elschen, do write more detailed and soon. All of you receive my regards from your loving mother

My dear loved ones, I don't want to let mother's letter go without sending you regards and kisses

Meta

Dessau   26 September 1941

My dear Elschen,

Enclosed the consoling letters from the children. You can be satisfied with them. Edith is trying to do too much. Hopefully she will learn to do one thing properly. The Jewish holidays passed quietly with peaceful nights. The reason for not being able to see you makes me very sad. Meta received your letter today and thanks you very much. Please give my regards to Aunt Toni. Meta carries on without hindrance. Is Willy still on the sick list? Otherwise there is nothing else of importance. I am fairly well. Be greeted and kissed all of you,

    Your faithful   mother.

A letter from Gert to our parents. (via Palestine)

Dear Uncle Willy and dear Aunt Else,   3 July 1941

I was very happy to receive a letter from you. I am very well and Edith also. How are you? I learn well, here. We are having holidays at the moment and I am spending them in the country and it is good. The food is also very good. I have just been given a shirt. When it rains I play Billiards and Table Tennis. Many regards and kisses to all at home,

Your faithful nephew

Gert

These are two letters from Frau Nickel, who with her half-Jewish son was billeted on my grandparents from early on in 1939. She lost her son at the Russian front during the war.

My grandmother 'left' her the house in Dessau on the understanding that she returned it to her grandchildren after the war. As far as I understand, she did not do this. Uncle Hans had a correspondence with her after the war, which did not result in anything. The house in Cavalier Strasse was bombed during the war. When Stefan, Len and I visited Dessau in the early 1970's I could not even recognise the street. The two letters survived, because I sent them to James in 1947. He returned them in the spring of 1990.

Post War..

Hulda Nickel, Dessau, Haideburg, Holunderveg 24,
Provinz Sachsen Russische Besatzungszohne – Deutschland

(from the envelope)

Letter 1, which arrived 14 August 1947   Dessau 27 July 1947

My dear Edith,

Please excuse me for not having written to you. The picture of you is delightful. You have changed into a pretty girl. Little Gert is now grown up (ein grosser Mensch). If the parents could have seen you, they would have been proud.. Mutti once said to someone: 'Even if we are not alive anymore, our children shall live.' No, little Edith, Mutti was sent away in 1943 to Auschwitz. Vati went a long time before to Buchenwald. Vati wrote to me and asked for warm clothing, which I sent him. I heard nothing from Mutti. When she was taken with Jewish help to the Grosse Hamburger Strasse, she managed to write a few words to me, to say farewell, and asked me to make contact with you. I feel faint when I think about it.

I have been very ill, that is why I have not written. I am waiting for news from your uncle in Palestine; did he get my letter? Have you made contact with your arian (non-Jewish) – relations? They have all the linen, Mutti's clothes and furs. I need legal powers from you to find out about the silver. They wrote (Elizabeth Johannes) that I was not entitled to have any information. I asked Rosi as well, perhaps you could all get together. I don't know how things are with you. I have to go to Berlin on Rosi's behalf and want to go to your relations on your behalf. But I have not their address. They were so mean and did not give Mutti any of the things she needed ..... It is very hot here and the nourishment (food) is bad. I hope that it is much better for you there. I asked Rosi for a few things. Perhaps you could send me some plasters, a little cream and some bandages. If you cut your finger here, there is nothing to cover it. To save on stamps, perhaps you (Rosi and I) could send it together. Sewing silk and yarn and mending wool are not to be had. Is everything rationed with you? I cannot get anything sewn, as there is no one to do it, even if you have an old dress.

For today regards to you and Gert,

Yours Hulda Nickel

There is nothing to be had here. I am prepared to go without, but all the others should also be without.

Letter 2   Dessau 5 December 1947

Dear Edith,

Receive a thousand thanks for your beautiful parcel. I asked you not to go to so much trouble and expense, and yet you did. I was surprised not to have had an answer to my letter of the 27 July. I can imagine that you are very busy. Today I will give you the address of Frau Johannes, who has the silver. The beast wrote me such a disgusting letter, and as soon as we have retrieved the silver, I shall get at her legally. I have asked her repeatedly if she still has it and she answered that she does not believe that I had any legal right to represent Else's children; especially as I did not give her your address. Then, she did not answer until I sent a registered letter and told her that I would take legal action. She then wrote to me, to tell me, how close she had been to the Gutman's. But when Mutti wrote and asked her to meet her, she refused first, but then later met her for two minutes at the railway station in Dessau. But then she did not give the silver. Her husband was in the party and she could not meet anymore.

Thank God, he has been dismissed from his job. We wanted to give it someone else, if so we would have it now. Well, she will have to give it back. And I believe that the Berlin Jewish Community can do it. Do discuss it with the others, if they will give me the legal right, or they shall send it to the Berlin Jewish Authority.

Her address is:
Frau Elsbeth Johannes
19 Ballenstadt Harz
Breitscheidt Platz 16, Floor 1

For today hearty greetings

    Your Hulda Nickel

When you write to her, make believe that you know from Mutti that she has the silver, otherwise she will deny it, as I am the only one who knows.

Letter from a former housekeeper of Gerda Cohen, a cousin of my mother. Gerda Cohen left Germany and lived in London. I visited her after the war, but lost touch with the family, as I did with others. It was difficult being on one's own without encouragement from the others.

This letter from Fraulein Bussinius, was written to me after Gerda Cohen gave me her address. The envelope and address were lost. I sent the letter on to America to my cousin James Falkenburg. The letter and the two others were returned to me in the Spring of 1990.

Berlin the 3 Advent 1947
To: Nurse E. Jacobowitz
Farnborough Hospital
Kent.

Dear Sister Edith,

Cordial thanks for your dear lines; just think, I always imagined that you would write. I am so glad that all is so well with you and that you have such a wonderful occupation, to help suffering humanity, as a chosen profession.

How happy your dear parents would be to know that their Edith is doing so well. We often spoke about you and Gerhardt, who was such a pleasant boy. I still see him, when Mucky (her charge?) was ill one time and I was sitting at her bed, telling her fairy tales.. Mucky, the dear loving creature, was also taken from us (died or deported?) and it took a long time before I got over the death of my darling.

Yes, dear Sister Edith, you were children then, when you parted from your parents with a heavy heart. Today you are adults who have gone through the storms of life, which has treated you badly. What misery and despair your people have suffered, and that I was able to take part in easing their lives, pleases me today. I took fruit and sweets to them secretly, whenever I was allocated my rations. Most Sundays early, when everyone was asleep, I went on my way and on a special bell ring it (the door) was opened to me. It was very difficult to help, for if I had been caught, it would have cost my head. But I always thought that God would save and help me, He, the God of all, Jews and Christians. I put the goods down quickly, in case of a search, so I could get away quickly. Suddenly, they (Tante Hertha, Mutti and Vati) had to leave Erdener Strasse and an SS man moved into the flat; which he had redecorated at her (Tante Hertha's) expense. They moved to Sybel Strasse. In the meantime Vati was fetched, for a few days, so they said ...... Mutti asked me to find out where he was. I found out that he had been sent to the Polish border with other poor souls (Schicksals Genossen). He took only a small bag with him and we never heard from him again. In the seven room flat, at Sybel Strasse, Tante Hertha had a front room facing the Lyceum. I think the flat number was 66, Floor 2. Mutti had a beautiful large back bedroom. In all the other rooms were other people (Schicksals Genossen). Mutti had to work at a factory in Weissensee for eleven hours, very hard. One week during the day, the other during the night. She was an intensely diligent and rare human being. Outside, as well as inside, never a complaint passed her lips. She always said: "Dear Miss Martha, it is not the people that hate us, it is mainly the party, the SS. My working colleagues are so nice and help when they can."

She was not allowed to sit down, either on the tram or elsewhere. But when she came from her hard work, the conductor (on the tram) said quietly: 'Do sit down.' Also at the police station they were polite and helpful. I used to get on my clothing card whatever she needed. Everyone was allowed three pairs of stockings (not Jews). Everything had to be ready when the day of arrest came. From curtains, Mutti and Tante Hertha had bags made, so they were easy to carry.

Much thought went into it. I managed to get them some medicines, as they were not able to get any. Tante Hertha was fetched away one Wednesday, right after dinner. I had promised to get Mutti warm shoes and stockings and something to eat. So I went to Potzdam on Saturday early, where it was possible to buy without ration marks. There were farm carts from villages and you could get everything there. I was happy to get red cabbage, cauliflower, celery and fruit. Sunday, in the early hours, I made my way to Mutti, dear Sister Edith, and when I came to the door, I found it sealed ....

I went up into the loft of the house, sat on the steps and cried bitterly ...... Collected on Saturday and she was waiting for warm shoes. I was incapable for days .... she had gone, such a good courageous brave being. It was too much for me. How often had I written to the Cohen's what a wonderful person she was and how I honoured her. That your parents had lessons tailoring, because they wanted to earn their living that way, when they were together with the children. Everything turned out differently.

Great sorrow has now entered our lives, but I will not complain, God will not forgive. We must all take responsibility, hunger, we cannot even wash, many people have nothing to wear. Cohen's do much for me. I know in England too, everything is scarce, yet they share with me.

Your grandmother from Dessau became sick and was brought here. And died here. Unfortunately I do not know her grave. Or I could visit it when I visit grandma Cohen's. What was her maiden name?

Now, dear Sister Edith, I would be happy if you would write again. Please remember that you have one motherly friend in Germany. Please give Gerhardt my best wishes. I will write to you about my daily work next time. For today all the best regards

Yours Martha Bussinius

(She died not long after this)

POSTSCRIPT:

Sometime before this date, I cannot now remember why, I had met the youngest son of this friend of my mother's as a prisoner of war. In spite of what I told the staff in the hospital where he happened to be a patient, they insisted that the likes of me be used to translate to Germans. 'It is your country they are from, and the war is over!' So this coincidence had occurred and at his request I had written to his mother, hoping that perhaps she had helped mine. I had sent some of my meagre rations as well for the same reason. This is the last and only full length letter I received from my mother's childhood friend. I knew the lady as a child and can vouch for what is in the content.

(Translated as near as possible.)

19 Ballenstadt-Harz 12 April 1948
Breidscheidt Platz 161

My dear Edith,

Today is the 53rd birthday of your dear mother. In front of me is her picture, which I hope to send to you. With great sadness do I think of the best friend of my youth, with whom I felt as one till the last days of her life. My memory goes back a long, long time, when in early years we had connections as children. As I recall a little four year old girl, as both parents took us to school, or better Kindergarten. There we sat together at first under a big flowering lilac tree. I remember it well. I was given a big 'Zuckertuete' by an aunt, but not your mother and so she cried. So I gave her half of it and from then on we were friends. The aunt often told me about it. We spent thoughtless childhood years and then went to school together. My mother, as we moved up in the school, always requested that we stay together. We did our schoolwork together, played in the sun, they used to call us inseparable. At times, we even wore the same clothes from the shop of your dear grandfather, whose immaculate behaviour and decent business impressed us all.. Whenever we made a family outing, your mother came too. Without Else Gutman, there was nothing doing. In the home of your grandparents I was able to observe a busy devoted life. I was often a witness at the celebration of their religious customs and could never understand that there were even then people who made vicious remarks about my girlfriend's belonging to the Jewish religion. When I became engaged at the age of eighteen years, Else was crying. But my fiancée took heed of my friendship and we made sure that Else was the first bridesmaid at our wedding and stood behind us at the altar. And it was she who held my bouquet, when we exchanged our rings. Your mother was working in a bank in those days and acquired a lot of business experience. When she became engaged to your father, I was the first one to congratulate her. I also went to her wedding in Berlin, it was wonderful. Your parents were very happy. I visited them often when they were living at Wieland Strasse in Charlottenburg. Every Sunday your father used to instruct the gardener to fill the flat with flowers, and gave your mother lovely chocolates. Your parents were well off in those days. Your father was working with an uncle, from whom he parted unfortunately later. He then started his own business, which was flourishing at first. But during the coming years conditions made him retrench. Your mother had a difficult time of it, and I often wondered how she managed to overcome all the difficulties during the hate campaign against the Jews, such a delicate woman. And how she stood beside your father during all the difficulties in the business. Your brother Ernst was born during the most prosperous time of your parents. His death pained your mother very much. I was very happy to hear about your birth. I remember making up a sweet little parcel for you and your mother. Everything had silk ribbons and poetry. Your mother was very happy to receive it and her letter in answer was kept by me for a long time. You were an attractive child, dear Edith. I can still see you, in your light long green dressing gown, a doll in one arm, as you were running through the rooms in your flat, and sat down in your favourite place under the concert piano. You had dark skin and very curly black hair, and your mother used to laugh and call you her negro baby. Your parents kept a nurse for you who often had difficulty managing you. It was very difficult to get you to eat. No, you never swallowed your bits. I can still hear the nurse: 'Now swallow it down, Edithchen, be good'. I often used the same words with my grandchildren. Then your little brother Gert arrived. He was a temperamental little chap, and used to cry often. Today, I am sure, he is a gentleman. I am so pleased for you, dear Edith, that you have your brother, and therefore are not alone in the world. With all my heart I hope that you are near to each other and understand each other side by side.

I thank you very much for your letter of 31 March and your picture. I cannot say little Edith anymore, you are now a lady. The picture is very good. I think you look like your grandfather, around the eyes especially. But your hair is like your mother's. I used to comb it for her. That you have passed your exams, I congratulate you. You will be pleased to finish it all. I hope that you recuperated well in the country. Martin (her son) is hopefully well on his way to Germany. He wrote of you to me. I am so glad you understood each other so well. It made us so happy that you were able to send a parcel to our grandson. You do not know, dear Edith, what it means for us. I feel that the world wants to starve all the German people. Unfortunately, the punishment is mostly felt by the innocents. I thank you and the Sister very much and hope it will soon be possible to reimburse you. It is most kind that the Sister is writing to New Zealand for us. Please tell her that I thank her from the bottom of my heart. As soon as we are able, we shall send money to New Zealand. It is bitter for us to accept help from strangers. You have no idea, what life is like here. If we did not have our children or grandchildren .... I would like to send you books, if one could get them. We have lost all our books during the air raids. You asked me what your mother gave me for you? Please wait a little, until I write again. I have to be careful. I know that you understand me.

Please write and tell me if this letter has been opened before arriving with you. I am enclosing two pictures, one of your brother Ernst and another of your mother. Next time I shall send pictures of our youth.

Well, my reminiscence is at an end — I have the picture of your mother and of you in front of a candle. I put flowers beside me while writing. We celebrate together the birthday of your good mother, my dear Else, who had such a loving and good heart, and who had to go such a dreadful way. But she will have been strong in dying as she was in life and her last thoughts will have been with you, for she so loved her dear little Edith

I put out the candle and give you both a kiss in eternal memory,

Your Aunt Elsbeth

5   A REFUGEE'S STORY CONTINUES

In the spring of 1946 I left Northern Ireland to go to Liverpool, there to take a course of tropical diseases at Smithsdown Road Hospital Tropical Disease. I had an idea to go to Palestine. At the time, many soldiers who had been prisoners of war in the Far East were in the hospital with chronic conditions caused by the ill treatment during their imprisonment. Most of them never recovered. A great deal of research was done at the time, especially on malaria. I enjoyed the hospital work and also my connection with the Jewish community in the town. The nurses' home was in the town, not far from the concert hall, where in nurses' uniform, it was possible to get cheap seats. It was a time when the enormity of the concentration camps was widely known and the impact put a final realisation of the loss in my heart. My intention after the course was to go to Palestine and offer my services. In the meantime I stayed with a Jewish family, even working in my hosts' corset shop, after I passed the course in Tropical Disease. My brother came for two weeks during a Jewish holiday, but had little to do with me, instead romancing one of my host's daughters. During that time, Palestine became Israel and I had the questionable honour of attending the wedding of the eldest son of David Ben Gurion, The future Prime Minister of Israel. Amos, who had been a patient at Smithsdown Road Hospital, had fallen in love with a pretty blonde nurse. His father came too late to stop the wedding.

Later that year, I left the claustrophobic Jewish family, they were trying to marry me off "for my own good" to stay with Mr and Mrs Wilton in Aynho, Northamptonshire. It was there that I absorbed a good deal of music and literature which nearly fifty years later lead me to an Open University degree. John Wilton was an engineer who had been in the International Brigade during the Spanish Civil War as a medical orderly. He returned with a medical condition of an enlarged spleen which had put him into the hospital in Northern Ireland where I had met him. He built aerodromes during the war, and contributed to the building research articles during peacetime. He and Mrs Wilton, who was not his wife, a fact I did not know, wanted to educate me. So my time with them was spent being introduced to literature and classical music. I earned my living at the Banbury General Hospital. John Wilton was a very sick man. I left there at the beginning of 1947 to start midwifery training in Kent, where John Wilton had a sister. Farnborough Hospital had a new maternity wing, where on completion they had forgotten to put sterilising units in! We were back to using big boilers with Cheadle forceps. Shortly after I started my training there I heard that John Wilton had died of his condition, which upset me greatly. The midwifery training proved to be interesting, both medically and socially. Until I attended my first delivery, I had no idea how babies were born, and neither had the girl, who shrieked as she thought her bellybutton would split!

One could go onto London on a day off to a concert or a show from Farnborough to Bromley if you had the money. My cousin Inge was by that time in England, having married the British officer she met in Palestine. They met in the King David Hotel in Jerusalem. She had the job of providing 'French letters' to the forces! She now lived at Potters Bar in, to me, a dream house and I was permitted to bath her first daughter. We went to see 'Annie Get Your Gun' on my day off. In the meantime after having finished my part 1 midwifery, I applied for and obtained a place at the Harrow Road Hospital in London, a London county council hospital for part 2 training. The difference in the dilapidated structure of the place with Farnborough was enormous. Water dripped into the dining room and corridors, conditions were near the Newtown Arts Hospital in Ireland. By that time I had my British passport, obtained with £25 with was saved with great effort. The lady who interviewed me was curious as to how I'd managed it? I was also in touch with the Communist Party in London by that time, through Mrs Wilton's sister. They did not admit me until I was British! My first and only use of the passport was a visit to Amsterdam to my father's cousin, Liese Hogenhuis and her husband Tom. She and her son had survived the German occupation thanks to her non-Jewish husband but had lost her mother and brother to the camps. She was very pleased to see me and I spent a pleasant week next to the canal at 17a Leligracht. I met remnants of the Jewish survivors, women with concentration camp marks, many who had lost children of my age. Uncle Tom was dismissive of the stupid British which at the time I could not understand. He just about tolerated me. His son Fritz was engaged to a pretty and competent girl along the road, Guusge. She and her parent lived in a house along the Gracht which still looked like the paintings you see of Amsterdam hundreds of years ago. When I left there, I knew how poor and how unimportant I was. Tante Liese sent me home with a new coat and some money. Tom did well under the Germans, but he saved his wife and son. Liese took me to Anne Frank's house.

Back in England I was sent to finish my part 2 midwifery training on the district in Hackney, at the Queens District Nursing home at Mare Street. It was a purpose-built early 20c home, cold and damp. The training was very good and our transport, the bicycle. I think we had to have 30 deliveries and ante natal cases. For most women it was the second time around. Meticulous reports of previous conditions, abortions and diseases and observations on ante natal care. The little box on the back of the bicycle contained all of our home-sterilised dressings. Once we were introduced to our case, our observations were kept and marked for our eventual exam. My progress on the bicycle was shaky. The Queens Nurses home was at the corner of great traffic and the policeman soon knew to direct the traffic when he saw me, nevertheless I made it. At night, the pollution of the time often made me feel along the wall to find my way. Most of the time a senior midwife was with me, but often I had to sit for hours to await a birth. Once or twice, the women would have to be sent to hospital if the wait was too long or if there was a post-partum haemorrhage. Once I had to evict a family Alsatian from the birth room. Another time the GP had to do a forceps delivery in the middle of the night, so boiling the fish kettle with the forceps and making sure the tear the poor woman had took all night! The GP had been up more than 24 hours. It was still foggy on the way back to the nurses' home. Shortly after this, I made my way back to St Bartholomew's Hospital on my day off, my thyroid had become enlarged and our hospital doctor had dismissed this as nothing, but I became concerned about the pressure on my windpipe and wanted to see a specialist, who confirmed my concern. So after sitting my exam part 2 (and failing) I was admitted to Barts Hospital and had a thyroidectomy, and as I had nowhere to go after the op they sent me to their nurses' convalescent home, Archer House in Ramsgate for four weeks, where good food and rest made me fit again. It was quite an operation in those days.

I now find it quite difficult after 63 years to remember the sequence of what happened. My involvement with the Communist Party for example. I went to meetings which impressed and confused me. The party secretary Dan and Hilda Cohen were very kind and had me stay on their couch in their living room, I had nowhere to go after the op. I had several jobs with a private agency, maternal and cancer. Interesting how different my status was in the different households, the worst in as German-Jewish one, where they expected me to do domestic work. Then one day I managed to, through Hilda, apply for a nursery at Notting Hill Gate which was for ex-refugee parents with children. Long hours and not much pay but all meals supplied. 6½ days a week, 30s pay. At the same time, a small room in one of the large houses near Harrow Road with one of the comrades became empty, which cost 20s a week, and that left me 10s for anything else. I was only too glad to take it. I fixed my part 2 exam again, which fell on the 16th September 1949, and promised to come to a party meeting after work. I moved my belongings and sat my exam I was not sure how I would fare, and cannot remember after all this time, but I passed. On the 16th September it was a discussion of British foreign policy and the foreign correspondent of the Daily Worker was there. So was another member, Len Bown, who walked me home after the meeting and we arranged to go to the cinema the next day. We laughed together and married after his divorce seven months later. He said to me "I'll get a divorce if you promise to marry me" Talk about romance!

During that time, I'd changed my job again and worked for London County Council as a clinic nurse. Part of it was a residential home in Banstead for orphans and children in the care of the courts, which still had gaslights in 1949! During that time we wrote letters and I used the telephone, the only one between at least 12 bungalows. Len got his divorce and we married on the 1st July 1950. Our only son was born on the 18 October 1951 with our love.

Appendices

Appendix 1

Reminiscences: Apprenticeship of an Alien

Written for a BBC programme in 1965, but not broadcast.

It is always an exciting thing to start a new occupation. Two weeks before I was 18 years old, I left the refugee farm and started training in the small County Hospital in Northern Ireland which used to be famous for the T.T. races before the war, Newtownards. The weather was bad and the grey stone of the place plus the grey skies were to have a constant effect on my outlook on life.

In those days there was no gentle easing into the aspects of hospital life. So, green as grass, full of love for the sick, I landed in the middle of it. The first thing was that I could not understand a word. The matron just about, but then she came from Scotland, but for the rest? The maze of Crete had nothing on the geography, though to my delight I found myself on the children's ward on the first morning. Of course, I could not understand what they said. Instructions specific, I was quite unaware that my place was in the sluice (babies nappies and all that sort of thing). But then they made me cotton on with a vengeance. There were children such as the like I had never seen before, with pot bellies and bent legs and arms. With burnt backs and fronts, lying in unnatural positions to ease pain and facilitate healing. Babies who looked as if they never had a meal since birth, and in a few cubicles cases of gastro-enteritis and an odd case of acute syphilis and gonorrhoea. The mother came to breastfeed the latter four hourly. Such was my introduction to the sick. Of course, as the most junior I was at everyone's beck and call.

The day started at 7.30am and with a two hour break, ended at 8.30 p.m. We had half a day per week and, glory be, a day off a month. As I did not go to church there was no Sunday morning off. My attempt to have part of Saturday morning as I was Jewish, were met with disapproval. (After all, we are giving you as an enemy alien training). I had really wanted the time to sleep and read.

I cannot remember much about the food except that I always felt hungry. That was not their fault. I was still growing, being late in that sort of thing. But the toasted crust with butter from the private patients were a welcome source of nourishment. We shared bedrooms during that time. A bliss after the dormitories of the refugee farm. My fellow student had already done her fever training and was a great help. The textbooks were most interesting.

The Refugee Committee had fitted me out down to the regulation shoes. They were supplying me with pocket money for the first three months. 'Mind that you pay it back'. It was £1 per month. To their credit they never asked for it back. The £1 was first year students' pay. It rose to the heights of 30 shillings in the third year. At the beginning of the month my brother and I went to the best cinema seats, and had fish and chips at the hotel. After that our prosperity declined. We ended up going for a walk and having 3d. worth of chips.

My progress in the hospital seemed designed with booby traps. Trying to be efficient, holding four bowls of porridge in my hands, I slipped on the polished floor and landed legs spread in the middle of the ward while the porridge radiated around me and the children yelled with the frustration of their hunger. The next thing was that the trolley itself ran down a slope and many bowls were broken. For this last lot I had to go to matron's office. 'I shall have to deduct this from your pay' she said. I blanched. 'O.K.' 'Nurse, that is slang'. . 'Right-Oh,' I said. 'Oh nurse, you really ought to know better'. What, I wondered.

The few lectures in the first year were given by the assistant matron. In the second year we had a sister tutor. I owe her a lot. She made me write essays, so that I could pass my exams, lent me books and eased my soul, when my position as the odd man out became oppressive. The lectures were a pleasure, except one was so tired.

I still spent my time on the refugee farm. Mainly to see my brother. But he was growing up by then. His school was in the town where I was training. It was difficult to see him and I tried to cut out a midday meal once a week to meet him. Someone told the matron, who forbade me to continue 'You need a meal, and it sets a precedent.' 'But I have to look after him'. 'No.' He still came and with the help of a conniving colleague we hid him in a cupboard. I was hungry, but it was worth it. The first night duty set a few problems. How would you pot seven toddlers in fifteen minutes, especially when they are not trained? I thought that I had found a solution to that one. There were plenty of soft bandages and the pots were tied to the toddlers' bottoms, either against the bars of the cot or against the legs on the floor. This worked quite well until the matron did an early round and found several small figures with appendages running up and down the corridor. Oh dear, I was in for it again. As I was the youngest student, I was made to cook the supper. With dried egg and no experience that was rather hard on my colleagues. They soon found me another job.

The ambulance driver was William John. He was a grand fellow. He did not hold with modern life. He had started his career with horse drawn vehicles. He swore at the engine as he must have done at the horses, and a pretty medley it was. He enjoyed a macabre joke such as lying on the slab in the morgue and frightening a young nurse. I had many a good journey with him. The one standing out in my mind was when I collected a patient who had one epileptic fit after another in the ambulance. William John drove like one possessed and I was coping with the corners and fits for twenty minutes.

Being the only Jew and alien in the town set something of a problem. If time for returning to the hospital was 10.30pm, mine by law was 10pm. The police station was somewhat barricaded. No doubt a reflection from the 'times of the troubles'. One policeman with two rifles flanking him was at the door. As for being an infidel, this had its problems too. The Rabbi had not liked me going to a non-Jewish hospital, and the non-Jews were determined to save my soul. After being threatened with hell (lovely warm place), I told one pinnacle of his church that I should like to go there, as I was sure not to meet him. I found much happiness in the home of a Salvation Army Major. He and his wife let me play and relax with their own small children with never a word about religion.

In the hospital we had our minor upheavals. One day a boy left the children's ward to catch a bus and go home. As it was visiting-day, his absence was not noticed for some time. Imagine our delight when a double decker bus drew up outside the children's hospital door and a lonely figure in a dressing gown descended. Security was increased.

In my third year of training, I was to meet the man who was going to have a lasting effect on my development. He was an engineer who had come to Ireland to build aerodromes. He was an impressive figure who stood for no nonsense and I was the only person on the medical ward not afraid of him. On the first morning before I had met him I found the parson running out of his ward mumbling something like 'Anti-Christ.' I thought 'That is for me.' John Wilton actually believed that women should be educated. Since I had left Germany he was the first person to agree with me on that. I spent a lot of spare time with him and his wife after he left hospital, and found in their company some of the consideration which I had taken for granted at home. He had leukaemia and died about three years later in Oxford. I was privileged to stay at his home in Aynho for some time and share with him and his wife their home and culture.

When I started nursing the only antibiotic available had been prontosil rubra. This was a metal dye which, when diluted, is used in eye infections. During my second year the sulphonamides made their entry. What a revelation. In my last year we saw the first septic cases treated with penicillin. I am glad that I trained during that period. I saw the miracle of healing. No more women were to die from septicaemia, in and after childbirth. No more sponging down pneumonia, standing and watching people die and having to tell their relatives.

I qualified in 1945. The prize for the year could not be given to a foreigner. The small market square in Newtownards was packed to listen to Mr Churchill for the official ending of the war. They all shouted with joy and all discipline was suspended for that evening. I stood amongst the crowds crying, wondering what was left for

me. In the second year of my training I had had a Red Cross letter from my mother saying:
'Now I must go too. Keep your chin up. Perhaps we will meet again'. In time had come a letter through a neutral country telling me to forget the past as life belonged to the living, to go to the hairdresser as a young woman had to look pretty.

I left Ireland in the Spring of 1946 to train in tropical diseases. It had been an experience.

Appendix 2

FÜR DAS KIND

Part 1: 2003 Liverpool Street Station

In the quiet of my home yesterday's experience seems unreal. With two hundred or so other old people I spent the morning commemorating an event of 64 years ago, which for us was at the time humiliating, frightening and traumatic. The idea that our situation then would one day result in a memorial and a celebration would never have occurred to us.

When we arrived in the UK, exactly 64 years and three months ago, my ten-year-old brother and I were just two of the 10,000 children who, thanks to human kindness and the permission of the UK government of the time, were saved from the Nazi gas chambers. For every child there had to be raised what today would be about £1,000, so that there would be no burden the British taxpayer. This was achieved through the generosity of many organisations and individuals. From the end of 1938 to the beginning of World War II in 1939, groups of shocked and exhausted children aged between 4 months and 16 years arrived once or twice a week in London, usually at Liverpool Street station. From there they were boarded out around the British Isles.

I often remind myself that British children also endured separation from their homes and families during the war, but they were at least in their own country, did not have to struggle with a new language, and feel constantly indebted to their hosts while at the same having to hide their misery and heartbreak. Most of us older ones knew only too well the likely fate of our families left behind in Nazi-occupied Europe, once the war had started.

Today there is a plaque in the Piazza of Liverpool Street station for all to see, with the figure of a small girl standing by a large suitcase, made transparent so that one can see the pathetic items donated by Kinder from their memorabilia of 64 years ago. They include letters, photos, dolls, garments and even a pair of boots with ice skates still attached. I still have an almost identical pair. My son used them 40 years ago when the River Cam froze over during his time as a chorister at King's, Cambridge. The statue and suitcase will be in the care of the London Museum.

Für Das Kind
Liverpool St Station

Both the Chief Rabbi and the Home Secretary spoke in praise of the generosity of the 1930s government, and also reminded us of the great contribution that the Kinder and their descendants had made to the welfare and prosperity of the UK. Bertha Leverton, who has done so much to keep the memory of the Kindertransport alive, and Sir Nicholas Winterton, whose courageous efforts saved the lives of more than 600 Czech Kinder, also spoke to us. Much gratitude is due to World Jewish Relief, active in Jewish welfare since the 1930s, AJR, RoK, and the Holocaust Educational Trust for the successful achievement of this event.

At the reception following, the gift of the Bloomberg organisation, I tried to talk to as many people as possible, although as I live outside London, most were complete strangers. Remarkably, though, I discovered that the sculptress of the little girl had a son attending the same school as my two grandchildren!

My son met me after the reception and presented me with a bouquet of red roses. It happened to be my 79th birthday.

E. G. Bown (Jacobowitz) 17 September 2003

Part 2: 2013 Liverpool Street Station

Commemoration of the Kindertransport of 75 years ago

Ten years ago I attended the dedication of the commemoration statue at Liverpool Street station on my own. This morning I attended with my son, his wife and my two grandchildren on a chilly morning at Hope Square, Liverpool Street station, in London. That little group of statues of five children, surrounded by the list of European cities from which they came, seemed so personal to me, reminding me of my late brother Gert and I, as we arrived on 21 June 1939 off the train from Harwich.

Kindertransport memorial, Liverpool Street Station

It was such a wet morning. In fact, it made us miss the train from Harwich. We were about 100 tired children, mentally exhausted with shock and expectation. For me, I was terrified that the arrival at Liverpool Street station might mean parting from my brother who, at 9¾ years old, had had enough of restrictions. And who would meet us, where were we going, and how could or would we communicate? My English was limited at that time. I had torn the skirt of my new costume just as the train left Berlin and my lovely blue hat had been sat upon.

The start of the journey at the main railway station in Berlin was on a Sunday morning at 6am. My brother and I were taken to the station by my cousin and aunt, neither of whom survived. My parents had been "taken into protective custody" six weeks earlier, leaving me to pack up our flat. No relatives were allowed on the platform in case emotions ran too high. The train went slowly out of Berlin right past a former flat of ours in Charlottenburg, and the burnt-out Fassanenstrasse synagogue that had been attacked on Kristallnacht.

There was the worry about my parents, who had been arrested six weeks earlier. All of us children had had our own anxieties, creating an atmosphere of restlessness and upset. The Quaker ladies, who had been in charge of us since we left Berlin, tried to keep a lid on all this. They tried to keep us calm and also the people who came to collect us, so that the handover at Liverpool Street went smoothly. The few lucky ones, who knew their hosts, were quickly dealt with. For the others the waiting was long, and at times full of distress, especially if siblings or friends were parted.

I had no idea what would happen to Gert and I. My father had said, "Look after the boy" when they arrested him in our flat in Berlin, and I had promised, a promise I meant to keep. The hall at Liverpool Street was big, dark and damp, and the seats were old-fashioned benches. We were among the last to be collected by a charming English lady, who knew some German, and who took us to her house in London to give us lunch. After 4 years my school-girl English was rather painful and halting. The lady was, although I did not know it then, the sister of Barney Hurwitz, the head of the

Jewish community in Belfast, and he was our guarantor. After lunch my brother and I were put on a train to Liverpool in charge of the guard. In Liverpool one of the Hurwitz relatives met us and took us to the overnight boat to Belfast. My brother loved being on the boat – it was an adventure running all over it, ignoring my efforts to catch him!

Right through this morning's moving ceremony I relived that long day, thanking the British government for the chance I had been given. If the 10,000 children, some of whom even became Nobel Prize winners, had made a good life, it was certainly right to celebrate. But it hurts to remember all these events and the people I lost.

++

The commemoration event at Liverpool Street station
11am, 1st December 2013

World Jewish Relief together with the Association of Jewish Refugees are pleased to welcome you to today's commemorative event at the "Children of the Kindertranport" sculpture at Hope Square, Liverpool Street station.

Sunday 1 December 2013 at 11am

ORDER OF SERVICE

Welcome by Linda Rosenblatt, WJR Vice Chair

Lighting of Memorial Candles by Kinder

Address by Henry Grunwald OBE QC, WJR President

Address by the Rt Hon Eric Pickles, MP, Secretary of State for Communities and Local Government *[due to illness this speech was read by Henry Grunwald]*

Address by The Chief Rabbi

Memorial Prayer by Benjamin Wolf

Kaddish by Rev Bernd Koschland

National Anthem

Hatikvah

Closing remarks by Linda Rosenblatt

Appendix 3

Glossary

Der Sturmer: Racist nazi propaganda newspaper

ES: Schutz Staffel, elite nazi organisation, amongst whose 'duties' was the running of the concentration camps

Horrah: Jewish folk-dance

Katzentisch: Children's table

Kristall Nacht: Referring to the night of 10-11 November 1938, when following the death of the nazi diplomat von Rath in Paris, synagogues throughout Germany were attacked. Kristall Nacht means Crystal Night, and refers to the smashing of the synagogue windows by the nazi mobs

KZ: Abbreviation for Konzentrazionslager, concentration camp

Mletkaserne: Large block of flats with central courtyard

Mittelschule der Judische Gemeinde: Grammar school run by the Jewish community

Mutti: Familiar abbreviation for Mutter (= mum)

Onkel: Uncle

Pessach: The Feast of the Passover

Purim: Jewish festival, refer to the Book of Esther ...

SA: Sturmer Abteilung, so-called Storm Troopers, a nazi paramilitary organisation trained for street fighting

Schwester: Sister (nurse)

Tante: Aunt

Thora: The five books of Moses in scroll form held in every synagogue. These are allowed to fall to pieces with age and are then ceremonially buried

U-Bahn: Underground railway

Appendix 4

Holocaust Day 2002 - Chatham Synagogue

The letter I am about to read to you from, arrived in December 1947, after the war. It was written by a Berlin lady, Fräulein Bussinius, who before the war had been housekeeper to a relation of mine in Berlin. They were Jews, she was a practising Christian. I can hardly remember her, but she remembered my brother and me. She kept in touch, at great personal risk, with my parents and my aunt, until they were finally arrested and despatched to an extermination camp, such as Auschwitz or Treblinka where they were all murdered by the nazis. My mother was the last one of my family to go.

In 1942 she had still been able to nurse her own ailing parents, both in their 80s, who died in the Jewish hospital in Berlin, They both died in their beds, a fact I have always been grateful for.

My brother Gert aged 10, and myself aged 14, left Germany in June 1939 on a Children's Transport in the care of the ladies of the British Society of Friends (the Quakers). The Northern Ireland Jewish Community in Belfast had been able to stand as guarantors for our welfare, They and the Quakers saved our lives. Something like ten thousand children between the ages of six months and sixteen years were saved this way.

Fräulein Bussinius acted with great courage at the horrendous time known as 'Kristalnacht' in November 1938, when the nazis attacked synagogues and Jewish property all over Germany. She protected her Jewish employer's wife and daughter by hiding them from the rampaging Brownshirts.

Her letter is interestingly dated 3rd Advent 1947:

Dear Nurse Edith, My heartfelt thanks for your letter. I always hoped you would write and I am glad that all is well with you. You have chosen a wonderful career in nursing, dedicating yourself to helping suffering humanity. Your parents and I often spoke about

you and your brother Gert such a delightful boy. Yes, my dear Edith, you were still children when you had to part from your parents. What heavy hearts you must have had. Today you are adults who have survived the storms of life. What misery and despair your people have suffered. I am glad I was able to play even a small part in making your parents' lives a little easier. Whenever I was allocated my rations I took fruit and sweets to them secretly, mostly early on Sundays while everyone was still asleep. We had a special arrangement for ringing the bell at your parents' flat; the door
was opened, and I put the goods down quickly and left without delay, for fear there might be a search. It was very difficult to help; if I had been caught it would have cost my life.

But I always believed that God would save and help me - He the God of All, Jews and Christians ......

An SS man commandeered your parents' and your aunt's flat, forcing your aunt to redecorate it at her own expense. During that time your father was arrested, and at your mother's request I was able to find out that he had been sent to the Polish border with other poor souls. We never heard of him again.. ..Your mother and aunt managed to find accommodation in a communal fiat, and your mother was made to work eleven hour shifts in a factory in Weissensee, one week during the day, the other at night. She was an intensely diligent and rare person; one never heard her complain of her sufferings. She always maintained that it was not the people who hated her, but the party and the SS, and said her working colleagues were kind and helped where they could. As a Jew your mother was forbidden to sit down in the tram, but when she came home from her work a friendly conductor would say 'Do sit down'. Even at the police station they could be polite and helpful. I was able to give her some stockings from my clothing allocation, as Jews were not allowed them.

Everything had to be ready for the day of her inevitable arrest. Your mother and your aunt made bags from curtain material to carry what small possessions they were allowed. I managed to get them some medicines as they also were not allowed to Jews. Your aunt was 'collected' one Wednesday night after the evening meal. I had promised to get your mother some warm shoes and stockings, and some food which was available off ration in the local street market. But when I attempted to deliver these on a Sunday morning, I found the door of the flat sealed. This could mean only one thing: she had already been rounded up for transportation. I made my way to the top of the block, sat on the stairs and cried bitterly. She went into deportation without warm shoes on her feet. I was distraught for days; such a good, courageous being had gone... Now retribution has come to us, but I will not complain, we must all take responsibility for what has happened. Now we are hungry, have no soap, and many haven't enough to wear. Yet friends who managed to reach England share what little they have with me.. Please write again: remember you still have one friend in Berlin who still feels a mother's love for you and your brother.

Appendix 5: Gutman and Jacobowitz Family Trees

Appendix 6

To Be a Pilgrim...

5 April 2011, 12 noon, I am sitting in the synagogue of the YAD VASHEM in Jerusalem and it is quiet and peaceful. Large and empty, surrounded by exhibits of reclaimed items of looted thoras, prayer stalls, thora cupboard curtains. Oh, but it is so quiet.

And I have done what I came for: visited the only place which commemorates my parents.

It is a plaque in a man-made cave which my brother had put there, not long before he died. The cave is full of such mementoes, hundreds of them, reminding me, as if I needed it, of man's inhumanity to man – and yet, I am here through the kindness of a non-Jewish group, who regard this country as the holy land.

If it had been Israel 78 years ago, perhaps my mother would not have written in Spring 1943 "I too must go now and send my love. Have a good life and remember, life belongs to the living" – and here I sit, neither to forget nor forgive.

I have viewed a memorial for a million children, and by mistake strayed into the entrance of the main museum, to be thrown back in horror by a room with an enlarged photograph of a 1938 picture, that could have had me in it. BERLIN, the ordered boycott of a Jewish marked shop, with nazis in front, like my late parents...

The walk through the garden of the righteous reassured me somewhat, because I could have added some...

The YAD VASHEM – a place and name, the memorial to six million Jews in the Holocaust was created on Mount Herzl. In 1965, the Israel Museum was opened, followed by the new Knesset (diocese of Parliament), both funded by James de Rothschild, who also helped to recruit the Jewish Legion in Allenby's army.

As I leave the Yad Vashem, I give a manuscript of my early life, my journey to Britain in a KINDERTRANSPORT, and my years as a student nurse, to the two ladies of the library, who accompanied me to the memorial in the pouring rain. My Jewish cab driver was scratching his head, when I gave him the card with the address of my hotel outside the Damascus Gate. It was in an Arab quarter. He rang his colleagues for advice. He was an ex-soldier, an invalid of two wars, who wanted peace for his children.

Back at the hotel, after lunch the manager came over. As my group had gone out without me for the day, he was inquiring. We talked. And it turned out that he had been at Wells School in Britain. As I had not been to the Wall yet, he instructed one of his employees to take me. He did not like me to go alone. So, through the Damascus Gate, the winding bazaar of shops to the wall, and the division for men and women. Amongst a sobering lot of ladies praying, I managed to get to a small piece of wall. I closed my eyes and prayed to a deity that had permitted such divisions and hatred, but when I looked up, there were pigeons and such relieving themselves on the top!

The next day, there was the Dead Sea and Masada.

I was a pilgrim.

Thank you, fellow pilgrims, and Nigel

Appendix 7   Gert Jacobowitz

Gerald Jayson

Gert Jacobowitz who changed his name to Gerry Jayson died on 5th July 2007. He arrived in the U.K. in 1939 at the age of 10 together with his 14 year old sister Edith as Kindertransportees. Their parents were murdered in Auschwitz. They soon found themselves en route to Northern Ireland where the Jewish Community had set up a farm at Millisle. Gert attended Millisle Primary School along with other children from the farm before going to Regent House Grammar School and later to Queens University where in 1950 he graduated in record time with a science degree. He was awarded a research grant in Durham University and obtained a PhD. In the sixties Gerry was visiting Professor in Burma on behalf of the International Energy Authority. The high point of his career was his appointment to the Chair of Radiation Chemistry at John Moores University in Liverpool. Gerry took an active part in the local Jewish Community being Secretary to the Allerton Synagogue. He is survived by his wife Sylvia 3 children and his sister Edith.

Robert Sugar from New York writes that Gert and Edith were the first to recognise and thank the Belfast Jewish Community in the form of a gift of trees to Israel. "We shared, though in different form, a great interest in the history of the farm and the events that brought us together. I knew he was sick but not that sick. He was a very good friend".

Gert wrote a most interesting article in the BJR 2006 about the farm in Millisle.   *Editor BJR*

Obituary, printed in the Belfast Jewish Record, September 2007

THE FARM

Sir – Regarding the article 'The Farm' in the February journal: for your information, Professor Gerald Jayson (Gert Jacobowitz) died in Liverpool in July 2007 having spent most of his working life at what is now Liverpool John Moores University, obtaining a professorship in Radiation Chemistry in 1991. Gerry was also past chairman of Allerton Synagogue and past Master of the Lodge of Israel Liverpool. He was a leading member of the Liverpool AJR group.

Gerry's sister Edith lives in Maidstone and I, his widow, am an active member of the Liverpool AJR group. Harry Gossels (Manchester), Felix Zussmann (London), Robert Sugar (New York), the late Rolf Dresner and his sister Helga (Berlin) were all also on Millisle Farm in Northern Ireland with Gerry. Rolf was the father of AJR social worker Barbara Dresner Dorrity. Gerry and Harry met up again for the first time at the first AJR Northern Get-together in Manchester in November 2002, where by chance they also met up with Barbara.

(Dr) Sylvia Jayson, Liverpool

A letter printed in the AJR Journal, April 2010:

The Farm

An article published in the AJR Journal, February 2010

Last night I dreamt I was ten again, on the Farm, with its rolling fields, walking up the 200 yards from the road that skirts the Irish Sea. In the dim skies above floated the whole of the Belfast Jewish community. To the fore was Maurice Solomon, the treasurer, Leo Scop, the chairman of the Refugee Committee, and the president, Barney Hurwitz. Rev Fundaminsky was also there in the clouds, attempting to restart my knowledge of Hebrew. They were trying to see how we refugees from Nazi Germany and Austria were faring on the Farm in Millisle, County Down, Northern Ireland.

Beside me was Herr Patriasz (in the early days grown-ups were still Herr), the Farm boss, frightening me with the amount of weeding I had to do. Then came Herr Dr Kohner and his wife, telling me not to look over the partition into the girls' dormitory and that, in view of my character, in future I would still have to eat a lot of dirt ('Du wirst noch viel Dreck fressen müssen'). There was also Herr Mündheim, glove-size 8 ('Handgrösse 8'), wanting me to cut an exact right angle into a piece of metal. With that I woke up and pulled the blankets back over me from my wife's side.

That Farm in Northern Ireland, on which I spent eight years, has held me in thrall more than any other eight years of my life. As one of the children on the Farm, my first four years there were spent at primary school in Millisle. When it was stormy, the waves from the Irish Sea would break over the road to school and we had to run to avoid a drenching. As you were coming up the track, the Farm was on the right, and Mr Beresford's trees on the left. You did not enter those woods, even for a lost ball, because it was laid down by the grown-ups that a Jewish refugee from the Nazis must not aggravate the neighbours. We might be sent back to Germany. We were the lucky ones who had escaped. I couldn't understand that. I thought, and felt, it was natural to be alive, even if there were Nazis and you had to be sent to a Refugee Settlement Farm.

Originally, my sister Edith and I were an emergency case, having been Kindertransported to England from Berlin. My father and mother had been arrested. Despite the fact that my father had been a volunteer for the Germans for four years in the First World War. We were lucky! In time my parents, all my uncles, aunts and a few cousins were murdered by the Nazis in Auschwitz. No doubt we would have ended up the same. But we didn't know anything about it, being safely taken care of by the Belfast Jewish community.

My final destination, Belfast, was decided by the fact that the Turkish lady who sold nightdresses to my father in his Berlin shop had a sister (Mrs Wolf) in Northern Ireland who pleaded with the Jewish Committee to give us a chance when the Committee were mainly helping Jews from Nazified Austria. In June 1939 the Farm was meant to be a holiday spot for refugee children gathered in Belfast.

Before September 1939 the Farm at Millisle had been a training place for young Jews from Europe to learn agricultural skills. Jews were not well versed in agricultural skills so the Farm had been set up for them. By 1939 it was painfully obvious that they were not wanted back in Europe. So the Farm, with Herr Patriasz from Hungary as a manager and teacher, was set up. Mr Patriasz, in his high boots, was a hard man, and looked it. The young trainees (chalutzim) were circulated round the different jobs on the farm so they could learn the details of each one. Cereal crops, root crops (particularly potatoes in Ireland!), kitchen gardening, dairy and chicken farming - all were given their few months' rotation. They learned them well because in 1947, when the Farm was disbanded and most of the young workers went to Israel, they cultivated barren lands into beautiful farms.

As refugees of all ages were sent out to live on this farm it also became a Refugee Settlement Farm. We refugee children were on our summer holidays and slept in large tents, one for the boys and another for the girls. As the beds were aired each day and the rains came, we never slept with the same bedding twice.

After September 1939, our parents couldn't get out of Europe, our stay on the Farm was made permanent, and we slept in more converted stables and the little farmhouse. A year later the large, long wooden hut was built and we slept in its large dormitories as we had done in the tent. It also contained a synagogue and entertainment/play rooms. I remember boys running through the sleeping quarters shouting 'Sh, sh, Larry's sleeping!' and waking the baby up.

The arrival of the refugees of all ages added nursery, health, laundry and kitchen training to the rota taught to the girls on the Farm. It was their child care training that affected me, one of the children on the Farm.

From 1940 onwards we went to the public Elementary School in Millisle with the other children from the village. Mr Palmer took all the classes at once in one large room and Mrs Mawhinney looked after the baby infants. I was ten but began in the infants because I didn't know any English.

On the Farm for the first few years we spoke and read German. It was only with the coming of comics – The Beano, Dandy, Hotspur etc kindly passed on by the Belfast Jewish children - that my English began to improve. The other children (there were about 12 of us), Harry, Robert, Felix and Maxi, had come over earlier and were more advanced in English. The girls were Sonya, Erna, Gertie, Annie, Daisy, Erica and Mausi.

By 1942 the young women had gone through their child training on us children several times, without doing us any harm. We were then placed in the care of Erwin Jacobi, an elderly saxophone player from Vienna, and, although he didn't look very motherly, he was the best child-minder of all because he saw to it that we got a grammar school education.

My barmitzvah took place on the Farm in 1941. While the other boys went to Bangor Grammar School, I went a year later to Regent House School in Newtonards.

Under Mr Mündheim's direction, the chalutzim built a byre out of home-made, reinforced concrete bricks. It must be the strongest byre in Ireland and will stand forever unless blown up. It is a lasting memorial to the Refugee Settlement Farm.

Every Sunday a part of the Belfast Jewish community would come out to the Farm to see how we were getting on. At this time we received clothing and presents. Naturally, we always looked forward to that, especially the comics. Occasionally we went to the cinema in Donaghadee - the afternoon 3d show. Our pocket money went from 3d at the beginning to 9d and higher. Living on a farm, you work on it, even when you're a child. Any holiday we were out in the fields. Hay-making and potato-picking were particularly busy times.

When the American army passed through Northern Ireland on their way to D-Day we discovered that there were Jewish officers, soldiers and chaplains chewing gum and chocolate. We collected metal for the war effort. At secondary school, I became a member of the Army Cadet Corps and played rugby. Read the English classics, took the Junior and Senior Certificate, and gradually turned into a little English gentleman. My sister had left the Farm to become a nurse at Newtownards hospital.

For all of us, that sheltered life on the Farm dissolved into 'normality' when the war ended. The chalutzim went to Israel. Everyone sought their relatives. Few were found because the Germans had murdered them. If any were found, the now grown-up children joined them. Robert went to the US with his mother. Harry went to Columbia. I stayed in Northern Ireland another few years and managed to persuade the Committee to let me go to Queens University and get a degree.

We Jewish refugees from the Nazis will always be grateful to the Belfast Jewish community for saving our lives, guaranteeing a £100 per refugee, and looking after us so well and long. We had freedom, food and a wonderful healthy life, in the beautiful Irish countryside. What more could you want?

This is an edited version of an article which appeared in the Belfast Jewish Record in September 2005.

Gerald Jayson (Gert Jacobowitz)

Appendix 8

Return to Berlin 1 – 1962

There is the story of the Children of Israel in the bible, who when they had left the country of Egypt and found themselves in the wilderness, remembered the fleshpots of Egypt only. I am sure that this is quite a natural thing to do, in fact most people tend to remember their youth in part that way. Last week I heard a record of the wonderful Marlene Dietrich and one of the songs she sang was: "I have a case back in Berlin, which I like to visit, when my memories make it so..." There is also a case for me, I reflected bitterly, after listening to this record.

In the spring of 1962 I found myself full with the longing to see Berlin again. It had been simmering for a long time. It had come to the stage that I was imagining myself walking through the streets of Berlin, and dreaming about it so vividly that it became an obsession. There appeared only one thing to do, get it out of my system. Every one of my friends and the few members of my family who had not been killed by the nazis that I mentioned it to, thought that I was crazy. But that did not deter me. I went ahead and made the arrangements.

I had left Germany in June 1939, with one of the last Quaker childrens' transports. My parents were then already in "Protective custody," a term used by the nazis for any type of arrest which could not be covered by any other charge. My younger brother and I had seen them arrested about six weeks before, after our flat had been turned upside down, and taken by Underground to the famous prison at the Alexanderplatz in Berlin. When we left Berlin my parents could not bid us farewell, and the last impression of the town was a smouldering synagogue. It was with this sort of memory that I was venturing back to Berlin.

After the war I found that I had one sister of my father still alive. She had been married to a non-Jew, and this had saved her. Her husband was now dead. He had been one of those who had earned his living helping to build the Siegfried Line.

I decided to stay with her. She lived on the other side of the wall, in East Berlin. I had no difficulty in getting a visa. I was warned at this end that Her Majesty's government could not afford me any protection, as they did not recognise the East German government. I set off on Friday morning the 27th April 1962. My husband took me to the airport. It was my first experience of flying. I think the whole journey took two and a half hours. When the plane touched down in Dusseldorf, I had an indescribable feeling of fear, near hysterics. We had to go through the customs there and then reboard the plane on the last stage to Berlin.

I arrived at Tempelhof Airport in Berlin. A taxi had been arranged to meet me and take me to my aunt's house in East Berlin. The taxi driver took me to Checkpoint Charlie, but refused to go any further. He overcharged me (I found this out later) and left me standing there. I went up to the checkpoint, showed my passport and explained that my visa was waiting for me, and passed through the border. On the other side I found an elderly man, who explained that he was just going off duty. He cleaned the border house; and could see me to the underground. The wall had been up since the previous August, and the station was some little way away. He advised me against taking a car. "They only swindle you." He was dead right...

The underground had a stop in Liebknecht Strasse, where my aunt was living. I said goodbye to my helper, and disembarked. All this time I had this feeling as if it was not I who was doing all this. The guttural German, the Berlin dialect and my own tongue twisting itself around unused sounds and trying to find words.

My aunt had gone to the Doctor, and someone ran off to fetch her. In the meantime a middle-aged man introduced himself. It was a cousin, who I had never met. Then the old lady rushed in, very breathless. She had been expecting me for the last three days. The seven in my last letter had looked rather like a German four. But there I was, and that was all. After coffee and biscuits we all went to report my arrival to the Office for foreign visitors. This was in a big building. Before you could get in, two porters had a look at you through a glass door. They then pressed a switch and the door opened. One had to show a document of identity, in my case the passport. In the office, which was upstairs, a pleasant looking young sergeant stamped my visa. Only then did I find out that I would not be able to travel to my mother's birthplace. Here again, the travel agency had misinformed me, by saying that one visa would cover the lot. It also meant that I would not be able to meet some other friends, to whom I had been writing for some time. I went back rather depressed.

My aunt was still recovering from a double pneumonia, which she had had earlier this year. She would be unable to go about with me very much. We were in the vicinity of Alexanderplatz. So far I had not been able to recognise a spot. Back in her flat, we started to talk. It was surprising how much I could speak, although their German, full as it was with Berlin colloquialisms, was sometimes difficult to understand. And I noticed that they did not even realise my difficulties. That evening I sent a telegram to my friends, saying that I could not come. I went to bed, covered with an eiderdown. Feeling very much away from home, not at all at home. During the night, I woke up several times. The stuffy flat, the unusual noises reminding me where I was. And it was so unreal.

After an early lunch the next day, which we had in a help-yourself standing up restaurant, my cousin decided to show me a bit of the town. The weather was not too promising, but at least it did not pour. So we went under the bridge of the S-bahn along the Liebknecht Strasse into Under den Linden. The scars of war were still visible, although a lot had been rebuilt and a lot tidied up. On a plan in a showcase along the road it showed that the East Berliners hope to have tidied their city by 1965. The Under den Linden is full of historical buildings. There is the isle of museums. That means that there are a group consisting of a national gallery, a history museum, and two others. Between them and the Humboldt University is a palace which used to be used by the Finance Minister. After partial destruction, it has been beautifully restored and is now used as the Soviet-German Friendship House. Where the crests of the old aristocracy and their weapons once surrounded a big hall, on medallion-like pictures one can now see the pictures of poets and famous writers from all the lands. This particular hall had been completely reconstructed and was now used for dances. There was an exhibition on Major Gagarin in a set of rooms. Along a long corridor, I found a big pleasant library. It had new papers and books. There were many young people there. I sat down beside one girl and introduced myself. I asked her what she was doing. She told me that she came there to study. She was a student, training to be a teacher.

Next to the Humboldt University is the Zeughaus. I believe it was formerly used to display weapons. On the ground floor was an exhibition of lithographs and posters, all of the last ten years. Some of it biting political satire . Also book-cover designs. There were also designs of frescos for the memorials of the former concentration camps. On the first floor was a historical exhibition of the German people over the last 200 years. Descriptions of the serf conditions of the farmworkers, of their inability to change masters. The influence of the French revolution and the general revolt of the labour movement. It showed the conscription of the people during the Napoleonic Wars, the sort of homes they had and the comparative comfort of the bourgeoisie. The whole thing was brought up to the time of Marx and Engels. Amongst the exhibits was a copy of the spinning Jenny.

As we went further on, there was the opera house. Next to it was a space, on which will be built a giant restaurant for the visitors to the opera. Near the Brandenburger Tor was the empty space where the hotel Adlon had been. It was very quiet along this part. As it was Saturday afternoon, most people had gone home. The Brandenburger Tor was about the only thing I could honestly remember. That and the Ehrenmal, which is the war memorial for the fallen. As for the rest, there was nothing. After supper, my aunt and I went to Volksbuhne. It was only across the street, so presented no travelling problems. This theatre produces a mixture of classics and modern. They have two or three pieces by Shakespeare each week. We saw a farce, written by a German after the first war. He fled to France and killed himself when Hitler invaded it. It portrayed a well-to-do family in England and their only daughter's adventure with a marriage trickster. It was well acted. The stage was very modern. I found that in these theatres, concert halls and cinemas and restaurants one is expected to remove coats, to protect the furniture. Smoking was not permitted in either cinema or theatre.

I was given two tickets for the first production of Benjamin Britten's opera "A Midsummer Night's Dream", based on Shakespeare's play. It was performed at the Volks' Oper. My aunt and I had tickets in the part used for foreign diplomatic guests. It was well done, long before it was produced in Britain. My aunt reminded me that my father had taken her to a Shakespeare play, in their youth.

On Sunday morning I went to the Stadtische Berliner Sinfonie Orchester. This one took place in the Metropol Theater. The conductor came from Tchechischen, the Prague radio. He had been there since 1934. He now travels about in the "peoples' democracies." It was rather a nice touch that he forgot his baton, and someone brought it from the wings. The concert consisted of a Haydn symphony, a piano concerto by Bartok and a concerto for flute and orchestra by a young Tschech composer. It ended with the Circus Polka by Stravinsky. The soloist in the piano concerto was a professor of music at Leipzig. Only in the last few years had he made the concert platform his home. I was interested in the movements of the conductor, who used the whole of his body to convey the mood of the various pieces.

[the piece ends here]

Edith visits the Jewish Memorial
Berlin, 2004

Return to Berlin 2 – a copy of a letter written to
June Richards, in France

Maidstone, 23 September 1993.

Dear June

I have been trying for days to put a letter together about my visit to Berlin, but am finding it incredibly difficult. On the surface it was a smooth, interesting trip. I dreaded it for months, because I did not want my even existence interrupted by yet another emotional turmoil this year. It was alright, while we were there, but now I don't want to remember.

Our hotel was first class on the Ku'dam, as the Berliner would say. The place full of foreigners, I heard very few real Berliner voices. We had a smooth flight and took a bus almost to the front of the hotel; as it was early afternoon, we went looking for my birthplace about ten minutes away. It is now a security firm, but near it were houses that the war and time had missed, so I could show Len the sort of place it had been. Around the corner from where we stayed was the Fasanen Strasse. There had been a fine synagogue there, which had been set alight on Kristallnacht, on the 10th of November 1938. I had seen it smoking. It is now a big Jewish cultural centre, has a library, restaurant and assembly rooms. I could get no one to talk with me. They were all so busy. Most of them have come from the East. There a few home baked Berliners. They are as they were long ago, East and West don't meet. Still it was good to see the old entrance door put into the new building.

Next day we did a tour of the city with two other Jewish couples. Both of them had lived in South America, and one of them now lived in Germany. We visited a former collecting place, which had a very graphic memorial. I nearly fainted when I realised what it represented: a cattle truck with squashed human beings held together by iron ropes. In front a huge metal plaque, as high as four stories, with the dates of the transports. (My parents dates must have been on them). We visited my old Grammar school, die Grosse Hamburger Strasse, now again used; behind it, an old graveyard for Jews and Thoras, now grassed over. Here was another collecting point with a less graphic memorial; 'only' a group of people, including children. We were in the former east of the city.

Berlin is a lively and attractive place. It would be nice if I could feel for it. But I cannot.

We met the representative of the Bürgermeister. A young ascetic looking man, (He had two teenaged children, was divorced, friends with his wife, and his girlfriend was jealous.) He gave us our pocket-money, advice, and booked us two outings. One was the Fiddler on the Roof, the other Cosi fan Tutte. We also met for lunch in a posh hotel next day and had a long chat about yesteryears and tomorrow. It was most stimulating. We had been to Fiddler on the Roof, the night before. It seemed bizarre to hear it in German, but both Len and I enjoyed it. We went by public transport everywhere, having bought a weekly ticket for £10 each. So there we were by U-Bahn, S-Bahn, bus, tram and Inter-City.

Thanks to Mr Nemitz, the Bürgermeister's representative, we found for the week a 'Stammrestaurant', a real Berlin one, to eat in. Berlin is full of all sorts of eating houses, not the least Burger places.
The day after the lunch, we got up at 6am, and took the S-Bahn from Bahnhof Zoo to Wannsee, changed train and went to Dessau, my mother's birthplace. It was in the former DDR. We got there on a double-decker train just before 10am. My shock was the railway station which in my mind was a little country station. It had changed into an ugly cement lookalike socialist

monstrosity. They were building all over the place outside, into the town. On the way looking out of the window on the train, the fields were huge, bordered by planted woods. The people on the stations looked very different to the people in town. Dessau is still small. We walked to the middle of it in ten minutes, found with help the Stadtpark, where my grandfather used to take me for an ice, found a little coffee place, and as the sun shone, sat outside. I could hardly credit it.

One side of the Stadtpark was bordered by Kavalier Strasse. At the corner of it had been my grandparents' house and the girls' grammar school. My grandparents had sold the town the place for the school! The school had gone, a block of flats was 'winding' itself around its space, the old house had been rebuilt and a big shoe shop, Leiser, was on the ground floor. Next to it the house had been spared and looked like the old pre-war one. It was uncanny! Len took pictures everywhere. The opposite side of the street is completely new. Once upon a time there was a theatre there, Dessau is the historic place of the Bauhaus tradition. Now there was a huge gap, where the space might have been used for parades during the DDR time. Indeed the street had been called Wilhelm Piek Strasse, that is why we were not able to find it in 1976; now it is Kavalier Strasse again.

Len suggested going to the Rathaus and looking up papers. The Rathaus, town hall, was a beautiful building, reappointed to its former glory, as was the square in front of it. I went to Information and was told that it was the day for weddings, not enquiries, to come back to tomorrow. Len prodded me, 'Tell them that you come from England and are going back!" - It worked, though the civil servant curators of certificates made a fuss. But then they became curious. So for the first time (and the last) in my life I saw my mother's birth certificate, and her wedding certificate. I also spotted, handwritten, the monstrous nazi entries of 'Sara' and 'Israel' against my parents forenames and the rescinding entries under the law of 1957. Len wrote it down, I was confused and distressed. I thanked them. But they refused to give me copies, as I had left my passport in the hotel safe back in Berlin. I then asked where the place of the former synagogue was. We were sent to an information centre a few hundred metres from the Rathaus. Someone came with us part of the way and showed us where to go. The person asked me if had been there before. I told him that I had spent holidays there pre-war, and at his request where I had stayed and that my grandparents were buried in Berlin, and my parents killed in Auschwitz. No more was said. We found the memorial to the synagogue, a simple white pillar, surrounded by a circle on which it said: From 1908 to 10.11.1938.

Being tired, we took an early train back to Berlin. As anti-climax, on our return I suggested, and we did, go to Kempinsky where coffee cost £2 a cup and cake £3.50. Len took a snap. The end of the fourth day.

Next day, Saturday, I wanted to show Len the district where I had lived as one of my last addresses, travelling the way I used to, to and from school. By S-Bahn to Alexander Platz (The Red Rathaus), then by U-Bahn to Brunnen Str., where the exit is almost outside the apartment house, where I last lived in Berlin with my parents, and from where they were 'fetched' away. And there it was, the only frontage to have escaped demolition by bomb or builder. The rest was utilitarian concrete. We looked at no. 115 Brunnenstrasse before we tried to open the big front door. It opened! The old staircases on either side quite elegant still. We went up the left hand side. I was remembering who had lived on each floor, then to the third floor, where we had lived.

Edith revisits Brunnenstrasse 115
April 2004

Appendix 9   The Pessach Song

The first time I heard this song was in the early 1930's. My mother and I had gone to Dessau for Pessach to be with her parents. My grandfather being one of the elders of the Synagogue, we attended the communal Pessach celebrations, the Seder, with a large number of other Jews. My memory is vague, but it all took place in a large hall set out with long tables and a stage at the end.

As I was the granddaughter of the most senior member of the congregation, I was asking the leading question at the Seder, 'Manishtana, haleilo haze' - How is this night different from any other? I listened for a time as the Chazan read or declaimed the answers and then fell asleep, head on table. They woke me up for the dinner and then, it being a liberal congregation who were celebrating, there was a kind of cabaret before the readings were finished. A rather well-known Jewish singer sang the song. It was sung in good German, I cannot remember if it was accompanied by a pianist. The song was sung in a dramatic way, but like a Victorian parlour piece. All were quiet, but when I looked at my mother, she was crying bitterly.

The song

1. Durchs Dorf geht ein Schrei
Wann fragt sich was ist geschehn
Es heisst alle Männer
Müssen heut zu den Soldaten gehn

Jankel der Schmidt küsst sein Weib
und wenn so Gott will dass ich dort bleib
so wein Dir die Augen nicht blind
und bete mit unseren Kind

Mein Kind soll beten für seinen Taten (Vater)
Bei den Soldaten ist er dabei
Mein Kind, mein Lieber
Wenn Got will, kehrt er wieder
Denn gross ist unser Adonai

2. Sie weint und sie weint
und schläft nicht so manche Nacht
Ihr Kind nur ihr Kind hat ein bisschen Sonne
ins Herz gebracht
Denk an den Vater im Feld

den plagt dort der Hunger und die Kält
Doch hat uns der Rabbi gesagt
Dass draussen sein Herz für uns schlagt

Mein Kind soll beten für seiten Taten
Bei den Soldaten ist er dabei
Mein Kind, mein Lieber
Wenn Got will, kehrt er wieder
Denn gross ist unser Adonai

3. Da kam eines Tages
der Rabbi zur Tür hinein
"Ester sei stark, Du musst heute schon
zum ersten Kadisch gehn"
"Kaddisch für wen grosser Gott?
"Ester sei stark, dein Mann ist tot" -
Sie weint nicht so schwer ist ihr Herz
Sie druckt ihr Kind, sein Kind an ihr Herz.

Mein Kind soll beten für seinen Taten
Bei den Soldaten traf ihn das Blei
Mein Kind, mein Lieber
Denn er kehrt nimmer wieder
'Yiskadal, veyiskada schme raboi.'

Translation

1. Through the village goes a cry
When people ask what's happening
They say all men
must go to the soldiers today

Yankel the smith kisses his wife
and says if God wills I will stay
so don't cry yourself blind
and pray with our child

My child should pray for his father
who's with the soldiers
my child, my dear one,
he will come back again
for our Adonai is great.

2. She cries and she cries
and doesn't sleep for many nights
Her child, only her child has brought a little sun into her life
Think of father in the field

troubled by hunger and cold
but the Rabbi told us
that out there his heart is beating for us

My child should pray for his father
who's with the soldiers
my child, my dear one,
he will come back again
for our Adonai is great.

3. One day the Rabbi
came through the door
"Esther be strong, today you must
go to the first Kaddish"
"Good God, Kaddish for whom?"
"Esther be strong, your husband is dead"
She does not cry, so heavy is her heart
She presses her child, his child to her heart.

My child should pray for his father
Whilst with the soldiers a bullet hit him
my child, my dear one,
he'll never come back again
'Yiskadal, veyiskada shme raba'.

Manufactured by Amazon.ca
Bolton, ON

44976830R00085